IN DEFENCE OF LETTERS

IN DEFENCE OF LETTERS

By Georges Duhamel

DE L'ACADÉMIE FRANÇAISE

Translated by E. F. BOZMAN

KENNIKAT PRESS, INC.
PORT WASHINGTON, N.Y.

18103

IN DEFENCE OF LETTERS

ESSAY AND GENERAL LITERATURE INDEX REPRINT SERIES

CONTENTS

		PAGE
	PREFACE	vii
PART I	THE BOOK AND OUR RECIPES FOR LIVING	17
PART II	OUR PROFESSIONAL OBLIGATIONS . .	83
PART III	NOTES ON THE ART OF NARRATION .	197
PART IV	THE CHURCH OF FRENCH LITERATURE	221

PREFACE

OUR system of culture is founded on printing. Thus it is not very old, for that astonishing discovery, which turned the world upside down, has been in operation for only five centuries. Books were in existence before the invention of movable type, but they were rare and costly. They were accessible only to a very small minority. Under these conditions they could secure the conservation of knowledge (not without errors), but they could not diffuse it. Then came printing, books began at once to circulate among the nations, and humanity almost immediately changed its aspect, and assumed new power and new purpose.

The man of liberal mind and clear judgment, who claims or exercises the right to criticize the destiny of the species, cannot but admire, as a whole, the work accomplished, thanks to the book, during that fragment of time which constitutes half a millennium. The book is one of the springs of creative individualism, that individualism which, in these uncertain times, remains the guardian angel of human society. For five hundred years the book has been, for the solitary mind, an incomparable instrument of uplift and liberation. A few decades ago there was reason to hope that, thanks to the individual conquests of the book, enlightenment would come to the great masses of the people, and it might be supposed that communal activity was yet to feel the influence of those high moral laws under the pressure of which the individual may transcend himself. The book, like every other human activity, is certainly capable of expressing and serving the two opposing forces which are called, summarily, good and evil. Nevertheless, there was ground for belief that the practice of culture—meditation, search after truth, intercourse with the great minds—would, by purging souls, gradually hasten the advent of true civilization.

But there has been a sharp change of direction of which there are many examples in the story of the human race, and civilized activities seem to be operating temporarily so as to suspend the very progress of civilization itself and divert it into other channels. Biological science gives us analogous instances of this curious state of affairs, and it is in this manner that the products and secretions of living organisms end, in an enclosed environment, by arresting life.

Various indications lead us to suppose that books, while still the *pâtée royale*, that is to say, the essential diet of the elect, the master minds, are going to play an ever diminishing role in the enlightenment and entertainment of the multitude.

Even though the statisticians try to prove, with the aid of figures, that the output of books is going ahead normally, I am still unable to suppress my anxiety. People who follow the march of events know that the book trade is in distress. More and more books are being published—I know that well enough. They are the somersaults and convulsions of an industry which is playing all its cards to give itself an illusion of vitality. The decadence of the book, the greatest instrument for the diffusion of knowledge, may be delayed a little longer; on the other hand, it may be precipitated by social upheavals. As far as France is concerned the evidence seems to point in one direction. The man of average means has to budget very carefully for his amusements. Usually he allots part of his budget to sport, or rather to watching sport, and if he can go to the pictures once a week, and listen in for an hour or two each evening, he considers that he has fulfilled his intellectual obligations. Reading a newspaper will fill up the intervals of travel—the spare minutes in the underground or the bus or the train. For the man in the street, the book, defenseless, is henceforward to be supplanted by less laborious methods of information and recreation.

What the economists call the "home market" is already depressed and disorganized. The foreign market is almost closed for political and financial reasons which are unlikely to disappear for some time. To these extreme difficulties new ones are added daily. Taxes, regulations—which I am not criticizing here—risky expedients and financial troubles all seem to be in league together to deal a death-blow to the book trade.

Some observers think that the book can afford to wait, and that when this tragic disorder is past and forgotten the benevolent influences will all be re-established. I do not think so for a moment. If the public gets out of the habit of reading they will not come back to it. We shall enter a new phase of our history from which there is no turning back. If the book during the next ten or fifteen years loses the doubtful favor it still enjoys, then it is definitely beaten.

I have often been told, and still am, that I am wrong to despise the new methods people use for their instruction and amusement. I do not despise these methods—I am afraid of them. I do not underestimate their importance, because I believe that they are capable of transforming the face of the globe that we live in and changing the harmony of our existence. I even admit that I believe, in the bottom of my heart, that the cinema and the radio, wisely handled, could yet work for the salvation of their victim the book. So let no one think of me as an obstinate opponent. The greatest service that can be rendered to cinema and radio—and so to their supporters—is to criticize their methods. I devote myself to this unfalteringly.

An optimistic philosophy whispers in my ear that the human race will emerge from this test, as from every other, ultimately victorious. Indeed, it seems probable that our species can overcome the worst miseries and the worst mistakes.

Thereupon my philosopher smiles and says: "The new humanity will find a way of being equal to the humanity of former days, which we have admired and loved." I should like to feel this complacency, but I cannot think without horror of unhappy experiences. Two or three centuries of barbarism do not weigh much in the scale of eternity. But all the same I should like to spare my children, and my children's children, these two or three centuries of unhappiness.

If events are still being precipitated—and there is no

evidence to the contrary—then our intellectual processes and usages may fall into disuse in the near future. Our moral balance, maintained with such difficulty, may find itself impaired. It is a suitable moment to take our bearings and publish our profession of faith.

I have written the present work not only to draw the attention of my contemporaries to certain urgent questions, but to make a deposition. Even though the publication of written evidence seems to be discredited, I have prepared a document for those of my descendants who will not despise the old dusty libraries. When they read me they will understand the preoccupations of literature between 1930 and 1940, and they will understand the importance certain spiritual and artistic problems had for us. It is not unlikely that such problems may appear to them to be entirely devoid of interest.

Although it is the fruit of long experience, this book is not a summary. I hope to live and to write other books about my work and my striving. I shall never have said everything—I mean not everything I ought to say, but everything I would like to say, everything I feel and know.

This book is divided into four parts. The first part only is devoted to the serious changes in our modern culture, and to the new forces that threaten the life of the book and the supremacy of the printed word, which is the sign in our time of effective thought. Before finishing this preface and passing on I want, once again—it is not the last time, I suspect, and I deplore the fact—to raise my voice against certain objections which, at this point in the discussion, common-sense people might well spare me, but which they sometimes level against me. A close examination of our evolution ought to be one of the first functions of the mind, especially in times of unrest. Good visibility, good steering, and trustworthy brakes are as important in a motor car as the engine. Yet things are in such a state today that frank criticism of the probable future is considered by many people, not by any means all uneducated, to be odious and sacrilegious. Every time that it falls to my lot to open a discussion on this admirable theme I see indignant opponents coming out of every hole and corner. In a style which I must describe as electoral, these worthy opponents reproach me with discrediting science and progress.

Future opinion, delivered at last from the racketeers, will, I believe, regard the desire shown by some of us to choose our route steadfastly and control our speed and our methods as being to our honor.

M. André Mayer, professor at the Collège de France, and a scholar of great renown, made me an astonishing confidence not long ago. "The laboratories," he said, "are working at this moment with splendid results. In physics and in biology, for example, we can predict new and very important discoveries. What is humanity going to do with the power which will soon be put into its hands? Humanity is not yet ready to receive this power. It is not in a state to make good use of it." The events of the moment prove that this power, of which we know very little yet, and which is announced to us with such proper reserve, has little chance of serving the cause of man straight away. It will more probably be employed, or rather confiscated, for the benefit of the ambitious, the impudent, and the reckless.

What troubles me constantly is the disharmony, daily more evident, between the inventions of the mind and the moral and social life. Our scholars are a thousand years in advance of our institutions, and the legislators are puffing along in the footsteps of the inventors.

For my part I am amazed and rejoiced at the manifestations of scientific genius. My great hope is that when they come to be applied they will not increase the present disorder. Not only is this my hope, but I am keenly interested in these problems.

The second part of my work is devoted to deontology, or the science of obligations. The reader must not look for a treatise, but for miscellaneous reflections on the life of writers, the relations of the writer to his public and his colleagues, and to his work and his profession. The last two parts of the book are concerned, one with the art of the novelist of the twentieth century, the other with certain characteristics of French literature and humanism.

I thought of calling this book *Biologie de mon métier*. In it I consider the life of writers, the development of literature, and the destiny of our art. Although this title was in the likeness of several other more celebrated ones, Alfred Vallette, with whom I discussed it several times, advised me not to use it, fearing that it would be misunderstood.

The title that I have chosen, simpler and certainly clearer, repeats, partially at least, that of a famous work. I shall be pardoned, I hope, since it is left to us to preserve the work that our great ancestors have so well begun.

G. D.

PART I

THE BOOK AND OUR RECIPES FOR LIVING

NO MORE BOOKS

WHAT would become of our world if some new disease were suddenly to attack paper and reduce all our libraries to dust? This is a nightmare question, but not an empty one. The word disease is usually applied to those disorders which overtake living creatures, animal or vegetable, and it is admissible to use it to describe the changes that take place in certain organic products, such as beers and wines. Whenever a living species in adapting itself to its environment changes its structure or its composition, the term disease seems to me to be applicable, and if the term is thus defined the phenomenon I presuppose is not improbable. Paper is susceptible to all sorts of physical agencies, but hitherto the biological agencies have not had any important effects, at any rate on papers of good quality. Everything depends, therefore, on some caprice of nature, some change or sudden variation in the properties of matter, which might enable an animal or vegetable species to live on paper and destroy it rapidly or alter it irreparably. One wonders why this fictitious hypothesis has not attracted Wells or one of his imitators.

I believe that if humanity were to lose its libraries, not only would it be deprived of certain treasures of art, certain spiritual riches, but, more important still, it would lose its recipes for living.

There are primitive societies where all knowledge is stored in personal memory. In northern Africa I met a completely illiterate Maltese trader who kept no books; all his accounts were inscribed in his memory, which incidentally was alert and surprisingly retentive. Men have invented books to relieve the burden of memory, and they put in books the things they most want to preserve. Memory is fallible; it becomes overweighted and bends under the strain; eventually it succumbs and fades into silence with its owner. Books are not everlasting, but they are durable. As soon as a man of skill has discovered the correct method of carrying out a piece of work he hastens to make a note of the operations, point by point; he enumerates the causes of error, the difficulties to be feared, and the ways of circumventing them; he records the grounds of possible defeat in the light of the principles of success; in short, he gives a recipe.

A library is primarily a storehouse of recipes and methods. A library is that venerable place where men preserve the history of their experience, their tentative experiments, their discoveries, and their plans. I recognize that history is concerned sometimes with nations, sometimes with individuals, sometimes with deeds, and sometimes with thoughts; in books may be found the recipes for the manufacture of a steam-engine alongside the recipes for daily living—the prescriptions for the mind and the heart.

If we were to lose at a single blow all the books under the shelter of which our fragile and complicated civilization has developed we should no longer know how to prepare certain chemical compounds, how to build an airplane, how to keep live-stock or farm the land, how to resolve innumerable problems—we should not even know how to cook our food. I would go so far as to say that we should have the greatest difficulty in using our intelligence to rediscover the moral law and subdue our passions, in fact, in behaving as other than savages or animals.

The great public libraries do not satisfy the needs of man. Most men, even the poorest, even the most feather-brained, own a little personal library which is the treasure of their own choice. Everyone needs a few recipes within reach. This is not only because books are the principal ornament of a house, not only because a book exhales a subtle odor of spirituality throughout the place it adorns, but because man needs reassurance against moments of bewilderment and hopelessness, moments of emptiness and despair. Try to imagine living in comfortable solitude, but completely deprived of books—you will realize at once that it would be a refinement of torture.

I know that these reflections of mine are going to provoke criticism. If someone were to say to me, "So much the better—let all the books go—let the world be purged once and for all of knowledge, and let memory be abolished...," I should remind him urgently that we have a hundred excellent recipes for rebuilding chaos today, and that despair itself must have rules and a vocabulary for its expression.

Perhaps someone will object that the danger is imaginary, and that the destruction of our libraries is very improbable. That is just the point I want to come to.

I do not seriously imagine that our books will be destroyed by a malevolent microbe. I should rather suppose that, as things are, man is likely to take the trouble to fight for his treasure, if necessary by transferring the most important recipes to some invulnerable material.[1]

I have drawn a picture to illustrate and emphasize a great misfortune. For this misfortune is upon us. Books are threatened not for the moment by a microbe, but by the indifference of popular opinion. Does this mean that people are less curious than in the last century, less eager for knowledge? I have said nothing of the sort. I suggest that little by little people are finding ways of satisfying their thirst for knowledge without having recourse to books. The average man does not spend much time on his spiritual edification, nor much money, nor indeed does he make any very persistent efforts of will. His capacity of attention and of leisured curiosity is amply satisfied today by various paraphernalia which exercise great attractive power. Radio and cinema are daily playing a more and more important part, not only in the amusements of the twentieth-century man but also in the visible formation of his character. A hopeless confusion is growing up in the mind of the average man between information and understanding, between entertainment and knowledge. The intellectual leaders of our time have not yet begun to give vigorous utterance to their uneasiness. Possibly some of them believe that methods are changing, and

[1] In Brazil books are protected from destructive insects in accurately fitted steel book-cases, which I have called "armor-plated."

that in future the human race will keep its recipes for living not in libraries, but on ebonite disks and gelatine films.

That is not quite the problem. The problem is not to know whether ebonite and gelatine are more faithful and more permanent than paper. The problem is not even to know whether it is in the interest of the future of creative genius to replace the book, that friend of solitude, by a number of appliances that are dangerously adaptable to mass propaganda. The essential problem can be stated thus: Is it possible to create and maintain a true culture, a strong and flourishing culture, through the medium of pictorial and oral apparatus?

II

CULTURE

CULTURE is at once the expression and the reward of an effort, and any system of civilization which tends to relax effort will suffer a corresponding depreciation of culture.

In saying this I do not suggest that modern civilization, despite its outward appearance and promise, leads to diminution of effort in all spheres of activity; rather is there a change in the quality of effort. The factory hand at the end of his day's work is no less tired today than yesterday. Perhaps the muscular effort demanded of him—and even this is not true of all industries—may be less sustained, less rigorous; but he expends nervous energy that is in proportion to the complexity and power of the machines he handles. The taximan, who drives his cab for ten hours at a time in all weathers, works sitting down, and has no need to expend much muscular energy, but he lives in a state of tension that long practice cannot do much to alleviate. At the end of the day I am sure that he is at least as exhausted as the woodcutter or the navvy, and certainly less ready for refreshing sleep and relaxation. Far be it from me to suggest that civilization absolves us from hard work—it frees us from some burdens only to load us with others. Moreover, the man of the twentieth century is oppressed by a bureaucracy which forces him at the same time to suffer its yoke and to fill its coffers. The most modest standard of living today requires a highly organized administration with all that it implies: red tape, schedules, office counters, proceedings, delays, disputes, quibbles, irritations, and mistakes of every sort.

It is an extraordinary thing that this civilization, which wears out our nerves and exacts an almost painful effort from us in all our doings, should be at great pains to spare the mass of people that intellectual effort which is the only measure of true culture. All effort is painful in a sense, intellectual effort especially so because its reward is seldom immediate, and most simple people are frightened by it; they prefer a long and hard physical effort to the unaccustomed gymnastics of the mind with their uncertain and bitter fruits. It does not need much to divert people from intellectual effort when they are already beaten down by the demands of a civilization which does not even recognize sleep and respite.

It looks as if some evil genius had conceived the idea of doping and duping humanity while at the same time flattering pride and ambition. I say "it looks as if," because I am no mythomaniac, and I am sure that there is no demoniac intelligence behind our modern evolution. But it is strange that things are as they are without anyone wanting them to be so, without anyone even being particularly aware of them; it must, however, be admitted that this state of affairs may seem to be due to the operation of a malign and resolute will. All the marvels which unite man in a brotherhood of the twentieth century, which keep him informed up to the minute of everything that is being done and said and thought around him, all these remarkable inventions which seem to have been designed, *a priori,* to make man more intelligent, to open his eyes and his ears, to stimulate his faculties and lift him out of himself, all these factors conspire secretly to suffocate him, to lead him astray, to lower his ideals and sap his energy. Charles Nicolle would certainly recognize in our evolution that law of compensation which in his view operates throughout the biological world.

For the moment, although more remains to be said, I do not intend to return to the cinema and the radio and the effect they have had in weakening the impulse to spiritual effort. I want first to draw attention to another aspect of the same phenomenon.

The press might, in our time, become a wonderful cultural instrument. Let us suppose—and I admit it is a wild supposition—let us suppose that the press should succeed in escaping from its economic and political slavery, let us suppose—it is a supposition no less fantastic than the first, but we will make it—that the press, absolved from personal motives, were to devote itself entirely to its duty of news and information; then it is not unreasonable to suppose that it could play a great part in the education of the general public. It has at its command every conceivable means of research and distribution, and in spite of its faults its reputation still stands very high. It could enlist the attention of its public, enlighten them, and to some degree instruct them, and finally bring them to books, which are the true instruments of culture.

But for some years now the press has been spoiled by a parasitic phenomenon which at first sight is unimportant, but which nevertheless calls in question the validity of the newspaper as an instrument of culture. I refer to the abuse of illustrations.

Pictures are acceptable. They deliver up their essential nature quickly, and they make us understand certain things that would be difficult to explain in words. Well displayed, in support of good texts, they can enrich our understanding of the world—some of our illustrated papers demonstrate that admirably. But in the daily press the picture is beginning to play a disproportionate part. It kills the text not only because it absorbs the financial resources of the paper and pushes the writing on one side, but because it has the effect of making the text seem unnecessary. "Why read a long article in small type when I can see at a glance what it's all about? I'm tired at the end of my day's work in factory or office"—so thinks the man of the twentieth century—"and anyway reading's a useless occupation."

Like a child, who licks his finger and turns from one picture to the next because he cannot read, the man of the twentieth century skims through the sheets of his paper with an air of fatigue and boredom. The least possible effort—and, however small, it is too much.

I do not criticize the art of photography. In the last few years photographs have made great strides. They are attractive; they transform, distort, and sometimes embellish reality. Photography is a great scientific achievement, but it makes people so lazy that I think it is dangerous and should be kept within bounds.

The magnates of the press cannot now turn back up the slope to which they are committed—they recognize that themselves. Rather than be reduced to the publication of albums, and in order to attract and hold the attention of a bewildered public which may easily become totally indifferent, they have had to resort to typographical devices. But we know well enough really that captions and headlines are no remedy, and that they only aggravate this terrible modern malady—the decadence of attention.

III

COMPETITIONS IN CULTURE

Can a flourishing culture be founded on visual and auditory apparatus? I have put this question several times to the reading public of the world and I have had a number of answers.

Many correspondents are of my opinion, that cinema and radio cannot suffice of themselves to build up a standard of culture. A smaller number, with less assurance, plead the opposite cause; their evidence demands equally close examination. M. Louis Le Sidaner has expressed himself very well in an article on this subject in the *Nouvelle Revue Critique*. M. Louis Sidaner is a man of great ability; he belongs to the generation who have decided, gallantly, to accept life as it is offered to them. Incidentally, that is the advice, in rather a different form, that I give my own sons today. "The danger of the cinema and the radio," says M. Le Sidaner, "arises from the fact that neither of these arts has as yet found its masters." He asks himself whether writing and printing are the only possible vehicles for thought. The answer to that question is no. He thinks that it would be premature on our part to pass judgment. We have no right to condemn the radio and the cinema, not even on the ground that almost everything they bring us today is mediocre or bad.

M. Le Sidaner seems to think in effect that my criticism of the cinema and radio is directed against temporary shortcomings of performance and technique. That is not my point at all. I am quite sure that the cinema will give us, indeed has already given us occasionally, some splendid works of art. As soon as a man of genius decides to use the cinema as his medium of expression we shall see genius on the screen—Charlie has already given us a foretaste. I am sure, too, that the radio, considered simply as a means of transmission, is not hostile to genius. When the music of Bach is broadcast there is genius in the loud-speakers. In this sense I grant the future unlimited credit. But thinking of radio and the cinema as instruments of culture I am disturbed when I consider certain necessary conditions.

Culture is founded on the comprehension of phenomena, of men and their works. Even a lively and gifted mind is liable to moments of hesitation and ineptitude; even an attentive mind needs constantly to go back to the data of an argument, to reconsider the elements of a problem or discussion. This act of going back in the mind in the light of subsequent knowledge is called precisely "reflection." When a man stops reading and says that he must "reflect" he means that he wants to retrace his steps and recapture a paragraph in the mind. This method is not applicable to the dynamic arts. When we listen to a symphony or when we see a tragedy on the stage we have no time to go back; only books allow us this deferred but indispensable "reflection." In the case of a great work of art we want to re-read it, to study the score so to speak, to see the details more closely. At a concert or in the theater we enjoy an entertainment. In reading a book we make a conscious act of culture.

I fully realize that, after hearing the radio or seeing a film, we can if we like refer to a book, but I put no great faith in this possibility. The spate of the radio is not conducive to reflection, that is to say, to true culture. The radio and the cinema offer too much—we never feel the need of criticizing or testing or developing or I might even say of understanding them properly. We take what we are given, pot luck. What we don't take, well—we leave! That has nothing to do with culture.

Sometimes the older generation opens our eyes—an old lady of my acquaintance gave me food for thought recently. This good lady had read practically nothing for some years, partly because her sight was failing and partly because her faculties were declining a little. Radio stands for the triumph of the law of least effort; but there are people who are no longer capable of anything more than a minute effort, and radio is certainly a boon to such people, who may have nothing to hope for from the future, or from culture or anything else. This old lady's family has given her a wireless set out of which she gets the greatest pleasure. The continual buzz of the machine dispels a whole train of sad thoughts and memories. But she has not wholly given up the idea of trying to understand what is going on, and twenty times a day she says to the unfeeling apparatus: "Stop. Go back a minute. Just repeat what you've been saying."

The heartless machine does not stop and it does not repeat itself. Apparently "reflection" is incompatible with the modern popular methods of soul-building. The cinema and the radio do not repeat themselves—they march on, they break into a run. They are, as I have said, like rivers. And what comes down these rivers? A horrible mixture in which good and bad are inseparably mixed, the worse predominating.

This brings me to the second point of my problem.

Reading implies choice, and the function of choice is a primary natural function. A living being is alive simply because it chooses. From everything in the world it selects what is suitable for its nourishment, to form its flesh and blood. When we read a book or a newspaper we choose our spiritual nourishment. When we go to the theater or to a concert we have in a sense chosen on the strength of certain previous information. Selection and rejection—we choose what we like.

The faculty of choice is despised by those modern wholesale distributors of vague moral notions—cinema and radio. In order to see one good picture we have to endure a thousand others that I prefer not to contemplate. For one good concert on the radio we have to put up with a thousand disgusting or ridiculous noises. The real radio-lovers, those simple people who really need education, are beginning to prefer noise to books; those very people whose cause I am pleading and whose interests I am defending do not bother much about the subject. They turn on the tap and drink, trusting to luck. They absorb everything pell-mell:

Wagner, jazz, politics, advertising, the time signal, music hall, and the howling of the secondary waves.

I assert, or rather I repeat, that a system of culture from which meditation and choice are omitted is the exact negation of what we have hitherto called culture.

IV

THE USES OF MUSIC

OF all the schemes submitted to the National Broadcasting Council in France ·there is one that has struck me particularly, not so much on its own account as for the light it throws on the problem I have just been discussing.

Someone had the idea of announcing forthcoming programs as they do in the cinema, drawing the attention of the listener to certain items, and thus helping him to make his choice. That seems to me to be a good idea. But the originators of the scheme thought fit to enliven the presentation with music. The music was to act as a sort of frame, by way of illustration or commentary or parable.

I was allowed to interrupt the demonstration to ask if there would be music, and if so what music, to advertise a talk on Descartes and the *Discours de la Méthode*. I must admit that the members of the council, all men of good sense, appreciated the difficulties of the arrangement and agreed to try something else.

Probably I am not radio-minded, but I seem to see in these absurdities a clear indication of the world disease of confusion. It only shows the weakness of the spoken word. The word is the natural interpreter of the mind, by which, between people of the same race, simple and effective communication is established; but that is not enough apparently; in future if we want to recommend a friend to listen to some verse-speaking, or to go to an exhibition of painting, we must accompany our words with light music, suitably allusive.

I am fond of music, and I am prepared to defend it at all costs against traffickers, pimps, and defilers. I believe that to use music as a maid of all work is a sin. We are tending to degrade music to the rank of noise, of a by-product; to debase music with words and to humiliate words with music. This prodigality is not generosity; this confusion is not wealth.

Habits imposed today are accepted tomorrow, and nowadays the audience at a cinema, in order to enjoy the moving pictures, must have noise as well. And what a noise! Anyone who hears a human voice will soon come to expect a continuous all-pervading musical accompaniment. We are drifting towards confusion, mess, and disorder; we shall end by losing all sense of proportion.

People talk about ornamentation. . . . I am not a systematic opponent of ornamentation, but I have a horror of the incongruous, the useless, and the supererogatory.

People talk about counterpoint . . . they say that the modern intelligence is capable of grasping the complexity of thoughts which are superimposed on and react on one another. Bah! Mere words! Counterpoint, according to the academic rules, weds voices of one nature, children of a single thought. Do not let us misuse these great words. It seems to me an insult to the human intelligence not to be allowed to say a few words about Spain without soft music from *Carmen* as an accompaniment.

Let the builders of the world of the future be on their guard—they are creating new needs. Let them beware of competition and over-bidding. Soon they will be asked not for clear ideas, but for more and more complex prescriptions. I envisage an all-talking newspaper, all-talking, all-singing, all-feeling, and all-smelling. Perhaps before ten years are up wireless listeners will hear a Racine tragedy with orchestral accompaniment, including a machine gun and a siren, while at the same time they will munch special sweets and inhale special perfumes relayed to their houses by the Government. What an intoxicating prospect for the delicate and the sensitive! Every modern convenience!

One of my friends whom I hold in high esteem admitted to me the other day that when he really wants to work nowadays—he is not a writer—he has to turn on his radio. The droning of the loudspeaker—so he says—puts him in a favorable frame of mind and ideas pour out. I cannot help thinking that this is not the act of a true musician. For thought has a rhythm of its own, which must either clash with the rhythm from outside and lose energy, or else submit to the outer impulses in restless slavery.

An acute observer of contemporary habits once said in my presence that the newspaper reader no longer takes the trouble even to unfold the leaves of his paper to follow the articles which, under the modern system, are cut up into several pieces. Apparently the practiced reader takes in everything at once, pell-mell, and yet knows what he is reading about. I must say that I have my doubts. If this is the true state of affairs, then the disease is really serious. We are in utter confusion.

The instinct to synthesize is a good one so long as it is concerned with elements that are capable of forming a whole. But today the man in the street is fed, morally as well as physically, on a mass of debris which has no resemblance to a nourishing diet. There is no method in this madness, which is the very negation of culture.

Last year I visited an engineering works in the extreme north of France. The engineer who took me round spoke in passing to a gray-haired foreman, and said in a friendly way: "I say, how's your radio getting on?"

"Fine, thanks," replied the man; "as soon as I get home at six o'clock in the evening I turn it on, and I keep it going until eleven o'clock at night." We were just moving on when the engineer asked another question.

"Tell me," he said, "what used you to do in the old days when you had no radio?"

The man hung his head and looked embarrassed.

"Oh, in the old days, I don't know," he murmured between the gray hairs of his mustache, "in the old days, I really don't remember."

This little dialogue seems to me to be full of significance. For many people, in future, radio will take the place of an inner life. Is this inner life to be orderly or disorderly? That is the present problem.

V

DRAMATIC FORMS

WE are at the "pictures" in a little country town. The audience is half asleep. The program is a gloomy one, and the *pièce de résistance* is a vague historical film. There is a plot against the hero, and we are shown the conspirators and the murderers. We see the daggers. The plot succeeds. We are present at the murder. Absolutely nothing is left to the imagination—real blood and real tears, and, of course, real cries, because the film is a modern one, that is to say, a talking and yelling one. The hero is about to die, and we are shown the wound. Is that enough? Far from it. We have to see the face of the dying man, the death agonies—close-ups, full face and in profile. Now we pass on to the faces of the murderers—a wealth of horrible details—the final dagger blow is shown from the left, from the right, from above, from below, in full light and half light. No pains are spared to give us our thrill.

Apparently the audience in this little town are impervious to thrills. They look on unmoved at these desperate goings-on. They are waiting for something more exciting to stir them up, a cannibal scene, perhaps, or better still, naked women. Or possibly they are not waiting for anything in particular. For my part, being free to dream, I amuse myself by contemplating the gulf that separates us from classic tragedy.

Is it really from a sense of what is fitting, as the textbooks assure us, that the great tragic writers have always carefully avoided any scene of bloodshed on the stage? More likely it is because those great artists knew that the spoken word is supreme in arousing emotion. Tragedy on the stage, in contrast with the cinema, actually shows us next to nothing. As soon as the pace begins to quicken, as soon as the shape of the plot begins to become apparent, as soon as the characters under the stress of passion have to resort to action, there enters a messenger, a servant, or perhaps one of the players. He is overwhelmed by what he has seen. He opens his mouth and tells his story:

"Il était sur son char..."

Do not suppose that in Racine's time the theater was mechanically incapable of putting a man on a chariot on the stage. Stagecraft was then already well advanced, very lavish, and very efficient. The poet does not bring us into the presence of the death of Hippolytus, because he knows that no visual scene can work on the imagination as powerfully as a fine speech, charged with pathos.

During the War I met a man who was of a strong and reserved nature. He was a doctor. The sight of the sufferings of the wounded did not appear to move him. In carrying out his terrible duty he preserved an aloof indifference, tinged with irony. Never a gesture of sympathy—never a word of compassion. But one day after the War I went to see this man at his home and to my amazement I found him in tears. He was in the middle of reading exactly what he used to see day by day. Had I not already known the power of the printed word I should have caught a glimpse of it then.

Someone may argue that the function of the cinema is precisely to show us things as they are; that if the cinema ceases to show us action and concrete objects it abrogates its primary function, and runs the risk of coming to nothing.

I do not know, but I doubt it. Sometimes one or other of my friends is good enough to tell me of a film he has enjoyed, and if he happens to be a good story-teller my interest revives, so much so that I may even go to see the film. I am almost always disappointed. The description of the film has made me dream, the film itself sends me to sleep.

When the cinema, which had so far been concerned only with pictures, annexed the spoken word we thought that it was going to improve, to become more human. The results so far are disconcerting, to say the least. The words of the great poets die in mechanical reproduction. In the films produced by modern experts words as a rule play a secondary part—they replace the captions, and are incidentally less easily international-izable. The problem seems to be insoluble.

But, of course, there must be a solution, and when people say that tragedy has nothing to offer the cinema I am not convinced. The cinema offers a spectacle, and the purpose of every spectacle is to interest us, to touch our hearts, to make us laugh or cry. But the art of the theater is more than two thousand years old, and we cannot afford to neglect the lessons of a history so fruit-ful, so rich, and so glorious.

VI

MODERN MARVELS

A CRITIC of our industrial civilization must not be surprised to encounter opposition; he must know what he wants, and he must know what he is up against.

When I am accused of belonging to another age, of understanding nothing about science and progress, of crying in the wilderness, of behaving like a mollusk, I am not particularly disturbed. I would like, had I time, to explain to such critics that I have had a sound scientific education, that I am of a lively temperament, that I live among young people, that I make adequate use of all the benefits of progress, in short that I am mobile and thoroughly vertebrate.

But reproaches of another sort can wound me. In an enthusiastic and well-meaning article some little time ago, Jean-Richard Bloch [1] took up the cudgels. He is a master of argument, and the political twist he has recently been giving to his writings in my opinion adds to their vigor and effectiveness. This is what our orator says:

"Radio is an essential factor in the far-reaching changes of poetic art to which the writer must adapt himself if he is to remain true to his function."

[1] "Nous sommes au commencement de tout," *Europe,* 15th May 1936.

In spite of myself I sit up and take notice. I feel that I am in my element. He goes on:

"Alain, Valéry, Duhamel, none of these men believes that the human mind is capable of adapting itself readily to the new rhythm of life. They contemplate the remarkable artistic fruits that the mind has evolved from the comparatively poor technique of the past hundreds of centuries, and they see clearly what will be lost by enrichment of this technique; they see less clearly what will be gained."

This concerns me personally—not me alone, of course, because I am in good company.

Jean-Richard Bloch goes on to explain eloquently that these modern marvels which men of my type cannot accept without qualification, will henceforward be effective in introducing to millions the masterpieces of art and literature. Unfortunately, this sudden extension of the audience—I am quoting Jean-Richard Bloch's words—instead of pleasing us authors, alarms us because we suspect "this public-meeting atmosphere," and—a more serious accusation—because we cannot swallow our instinctive mistrust of these "millions of anonymous nobodies."

No, Jean-Richard, you are on the wrong tack, and your eloquence is not consistently generous.

If I understand the argument properly it means that people of my way of thinking are dogs in the manger who want to keep to themselves the Fifth Symphony of Beethoven, the poems of Arthur Rimbaud, and various other treasures of art ... the idea that our aesthetic joys may be shared by an eager crowd is enough to spoil our appetite ... and so on. I know the symptoms of this disease only too well—sometimes it is fatal; it might be called the disease of aristocracy.

I will not venture to reply on behalf of my fellow-accused. I will speak for myself alone.

I will set aside for the moment considerations of the nature, the function, and the necessity of aristocracies. Aristocracy of the mind, as of the brain and the heart, is real enough. It is the only true aristocracy in my opinion. It is the essence, the very life of a well-built society. There is no need to enlarge on the point.

The function of the true aristocrat is, without forgoing his own faculties (I do not say privileges), to educate the crowd, directly or indirectly, to persuade them, to seduce them in the better sense of the word, in order the better to direct them. To this end many different media and methods are available for the enlightened minority: personal example, the spoken word, the written word, and in this century radio and moving pictures. All these processes have potentialities for good; their value depends on the ideas behind them. If it is proposed to establish a basic culture among the "anonymous millions," then I assert that the written word—chiefly in the form of books—is a more reliable process than all the rest put together. I have already given my reasons for saying this and will not repeat them now.

When Jean-Richard Bloch accuses men of my type, or rather of my station, of looking down on the "millions of anonymous nobodies," he makes me smile. I write for the humble folk from whom I have sprung. For them I send my printed messages into the world, and the more there are of them ready to listen the better I shall be pleased. They know well enough—at any rate those who are not already blinded and misled know—that if a way can be found, I mean an honest, human way of making life fairer and happier, I shall ask with all my heart for this way to be tried, and I shall do my best to help the builders of a less barbarous society.

I am fifty-two years old, so that I have lived the best part of my life. My boys will have to struggle as I myself have struggled. I face the future with a sense of great independence. When I say, "Beware of the radio if you want to improve your mind," I am sure that I am giving good advice. I am not being egoistic; on the contrary, I am simply stating my own point of view and recommending it. I am warning the public against their worst enemy, conformity.

Books are the friends of solitude. They develop individuality and freedom. In solitary reading a man who is seeking himself has some chance of finding himself; he chooses, and he chooses for himself; he escapes from the poisonous air of propaganda. Radio, on the other hand, is now the chief agent of imperialism. It does not purify the spirit of man, does not, like the book, bring him back to the sanctuary of solitude, but throws him to the lions, subtly preparing his mind for the blood and chains of the public sacrifice.

That is why I say, Jean-Richard Bloch, in the firm intention of enlightening the public whom it is my function to serve, that is why I say to anyone who will listen: Use your radio, but know how to distrust it— and do not let a day go by without reading and meditation if you want to save your soul, that soul which is yours and yours alone.

VII

RELIGION OF BOOKS

WHEN I analyze my memories carefully I can assess the part that oral communication plays in forming the mind. My oral memory is not exceptional, but it is genuinely reliable. I still remember, forty years on, some of the expressions used by my schoolmaster. If I listen in the night watches I can hear the man's voice with all its inflections, and even the rhythm of his breathing. The personality of a schoolmaster is probably more important than anything he says. He talks to young minds, still plastic and absorbent, and if he happens to have a gift of eloquence, a love of his craft, and a will to impart knowledge there can be no doubt of his power. In the intimacy of the classroom, that intimacy which is comparable to family life, the teacher uses words which will later become incorporated in new mentalities, to live in them up to the very hour of death.

A communication stripped of this all-important quality—the voice and physical presence of a man—might seem to be a poor affair, cold and without inner virtue. But what the teacher imparts by word of mouth is nothing in comparison with what he teaches us to get for ourselves from books. A good teacher knows where the sources are and how they should be tapped, can infect his pupils with a taste for reading and a passion for books, and can show them how to absorb what they need from books.

Many professors publish their lecture notes partly to give their own thought definitive form and partly so that their students can have a text to rely on and to go back to as often as they wish. When the student has no printed text to refer to he makes his own text by taking notes, thus fixing the phrases in his mind by the written word and making them available for subsequent reference.

I cannot say often enough that, as things are at present, the future of our civilization is bound up with the fate of the book. And I would add that our hopes for the future of the book depend largely on the goodwill of the university bodies.

It would be wrong to think that the case for the book is clear or generally accepted. For some years past numerous attempts have been made to introduce films, gramophones, and radio in the classroom—especially in the elementary schools. If pictures and talking machines are to be regarded as a sort of diversion, like games or holidays, then I am all in favor of them. But if, as their sponsors intend, they are to be used as new methods of instruction, then I insist that the whole question should be examined dispassionately by responsible people.

It is quite possible that a picture may, in certain cases, have a value for purposes of demonstration that is lacking in the more precise methods of reasoning. Pictures are indispensable in some branches of science, and a moving picture may well supplement a lecture, though it should never replace it altogether. But it must be recognized that once the cinema is installed it will inevitably begin to play an ever-increasing part in the collaboration. I realize that the schoolmaster's work will be lightened, and that most classes, at any rate in the cities, are too big at present; so that it is only natural that the overworked teacher should turn towards mechanical assistance. The cinema and the gramophone might perhaps do for the educationist what the machine has done for the industrialist—though in my opinion that is not saying much. The advocates of the system—I use the word advisedly—are simple enough to claim that knowledge so presented will make its way into the mind more easily and more rapidly. I say straight out that such talk is rubbish. Education demands work, real work—digging, hoeing, and rolling. Nothing can be acquired without effort, and the mind is not formed by sleep and play. It is right enough to laugh and enjoy life, but only as the reward of long and patient endeavor.

Let teachers who care for their profession permit the occasional use of sound machines and moving pictures, but let them be on their guard. Never let them allow the young people committed to their charge to believe that they can learn without recourse to the printed text, the book, the written exercise. The danger is apparent at present only in the elementary schools; but there it is very apparent. The day that the school-masters, who are our strongest allies in the defense of civilization, the day, I say, that our schoolmasters renounce the religion of books for their pupils, that day will be the beginning of the new dark ages.

VIII

BOOKS LIVE

THE present world crisis is not merely economic or political or social—it is a crisis of civilization as a whole. Problems of every sort raise their ugly heads. Cultural problems are, and must remain, in the forefront of our responsibilities. New methods of dissemination of news, of entertainment, and of education have become available and are springing into popular favor. Only the future can tell what these methods will be worth, but there is no denying that they have already revolutionized current practice. I am strongly of the opinion that these new systems should be rigorously and watchfully criticized, and I have said so repeatedly; but from now on we have to reckon with the effects of this revolution. The printed word is no longer the only vehicle of the mind, and the supremacy of the book is threatened. It is quite possible that before fifty years are gone, books will mean nothing to the general public, and will be confined to a small literary coterie.

André Rousseaux once said to me that public readings from good authors—they are given sometimes over the radio—might get people into the book habit again. I should like to think so, but I have my doubts. It is never right to push people along the line of least resistance. But I am digressing. Let us remember that reading is not yet dead, and let us look at some aspects of its everyday use.

A well-balanced man, of average education, needs reading just as he needs air to breathe or water to drink. This thirst for reading is so real and so continuous that we quench it automatically, without even realizing that we are doing so. Like a bird which all day long pecks with his beak at an insect, a worm, a piece of grit, a bud, a crumb, so the eye instinctively singles out the written word from all other visible objects. Such reading is automatic—a word that is full of significance for the children of the twentieth century. A symptom to be noted.

There should be two different words for reading. Just as we say "listening and hearing," "looking and seeing," so we ought to have two expressions to distinguish active reading from passive or contemplative. Passive reading is far from being valueless—it makes its mark, as the propagandists know only too well. Whenever we go through a town in a motor car or in a train we read what catches our eyes, even if we are outwardly uninterested—posters, notices, names of shops, and writing of all sorts. Whenever a prospectus or a scrap of printed paper comes through our hands we give it an inquisitive glance. We are always mentally receptive, or rather acquisitive, so keen is our need for reading, so strong is our habit of seeking our spiritual nourishment among printed words.

The meal-times of our feasts of reading are not fixed, but the bill of fare is familiar enough. Broadly speaking we read three kinds of things—newspapers, magazines, and books.

Books must be given the place of honor. It is their ambition to last forever. When I say "forever" I use the expression in its despairingly human sense; in practice if a printed thought is still alive after three hundred years we call it immortal or eternal, which is really highly incorrect. We know very well that one day, in the distant future, the name of Shakespeare will evoke no response on this earth. There may have been Shakespeares in the moon—and the moon is a lump of ice today.

Nevertheless, as I said, a book wants to live forever. It claims the right to a place in both our physical and spiritual lives; it hopes to live in our house, close at hand, under our eyes; it has decorative value as "furniture." Bound in fine stuffs and precious metals it is comparable to a jewel, and we look on it with affectionate gratitude. We are aware of its presence, and at our bidding it will tell us all it knows. If we knew how to ask it questions it would be ready to reply. To know how to use books is the true culture, as I believe André Gide has said in other words.

From books we ask what I may call the elements of knowledge; from newspapers the elements of news and information.

The newspaper is indispensable to the man of today. It opens his eyes for him when he gets out of bed. It wakes him up by throwing a bundle of facts and ideas in his face. It is his morning meal. It is so arranged as to stimulate the imagination rather than to instruct or develop—it titillates the mind, tells stories, expresses opinions. It makes use, increasingly, of typographical devices. It gives more and more space to pictures which demand no effort from the reader. Its first idea is to catch the reader's attention. Of course, it offers ideas and principles, a little literary jam, some philosophy, but its primary function is red-hot news.

For this very reason an old newspaper has no attraction and very little meaning. A paper once read is like a squeezed lemon, and it slips easily into the waste-paper basket. It hardly ever takes any permanent place in the household, and only rarely do we turn back to it years later for information or evidence.

During the last few years the paper has changed character; we have now the "weekly," which looks like a daily paper, but offers more solid food, and makes some attempt at a longer view in passing comment and judgment on things and persons.

It remains to define the function of the review. The review comes halfway between the book and the newspaper, and as its name suggests its duty is to review—to pass under judgment—a short period of world history. It exercises a sort of control over reality, and manufactures its own distilled or sublimated actuality. The dust clouds of past deeds disperse, and from what remains the mind takes its necessary nourishment; a real review should show traces of every important world event, should comment, record, judge, explain; and a review worthy of the name ought also to offer original contemporary work with some claim to permanence. It should be a microcosm wherein world events are reflected and classified according to their importance.

Such a publication shares the life of books. It does

not die at once, and will find a place on the shelves of our library, where it can be consulted at our pleasure. It answers our questions and reminds us what was going on, and how, in such and such a year or season.

The reviews are indispensable to the intellectual equilibrium of the countries that today guard our civilization. Gone are the days when a group of writers founded a new literary review every six months. The young poets sometimes try still, in a small way, at great cost to themselves—paper is dear, and so is print, and public interest is distracted in all sorts of other ways. To keep a review alive needs not only money and hard work, but faith and love and unselfish devotion.

Some observers come to the conclusion that the world is changing, and that there is nothing for it but for the reviews to fade out. I believe that this would be a great misfortune. The reviews represent a form of intellectual activity which is more than ever desirable in the present disorder. Continuity of thought, creative meditation, active study can only be preserved with the help of the literary reviews that survive. Books are clumsy and slow; newspapers are too short and too slick. There must be some method of examining and criticizing men and affairs, and for this purpose we need the review, which is the natural vehicle of watchful, tenacious thinking.

The disappearance of even one review, just now, when intelligence is being restricted in its function, would be a misfortune. It is not a question of one school of thought or another; there is only one cause now, the cause of freedom of thought which is guarding its rights against attack from every side.

IX

ON ADVERTISING

UNREMITTINGLY, with the certain knowledge that I am serving the society into which I was born, indeed that I am serving mankind as a whole, I tell my contemporaries that printing is a sacred art, and I warn them that it is in serious danger; that the taste for reading is falling into decay and that we must find a cure for what in my opinion is a serious misfortune for our species.

Mine is not a voice crying in the wilderness; other voices are to be heard, other remedies are being proposed. What are they, and what are they worth? Most of them seem to me to be well meaning but useless; moreover, quite unsuitable for the particular disease. The booksellers have hitherto been playing a lone hand in the fight against the public disaffection for print. From time to time I have tried to investigate the important question of advertising; as I have often said, it seems to me to have been ill-conceived from the outset.

The book trade, in the hope of reviving the interest of a jaded and battered public, has tried to do so by means of various allurements which are not strictly relevant. In order to sell books they have tried to deal in tea, port wine, cocktails. They have tried to turn bookshops into clubs where customers can meet each other and talk and sit about. I believe, and I have already said so in another work of mine, that a good bookshop should be a meeting-place, where educated people can exchange ideas and personal preferences; I would not want to discourage any worthy endeavor, undertaken in good faith, but I cannot think that it is right to mix up book-selling and the cause of the book as a whole, with social matters.

Then the vogue for signed copies has not improved the condition of the book trade, and it has put more work on booksellers and authors. I have several times protested against this custom, and it may be profitable to write a few more words on the subject. Books, and the future of culture, cannot be saved by signed copies. The only result is that the public now expect a written signature to be thrown in whenever they buy a book. They buy no more books than before, but they exact a service which still further complicates the work of the bookseller, disturbs the author and wastes his time, and lowers the prestige of a profession which flourishes best in privacy. The wholesale signing of copies has done nothing but harm to the book trade, and looks likely to become an incurable disease.

Not long ago a gifted musician wrote appealingly to the Paris publishers suggesting a new experiment. His idea was to attract readers by organizing concerts in the bookshops of Paris, and perhaps in the provinces as well, with the assistance of well-known soloists. One cannot help being touched by the generosity of the idea, but I must say that I think such experiments are not only off the point but positively damaging.

Think of it. The book is the resting-place of all human thought, the temple of all knowledge and wisdom, and to bring converts to its cause it is suggested that we must beat the drum and bang the cymbals, must get the help of singers and comedians and goodness knows whom—later on, conjurers and acrobats no doubt. Think of it. We want to revive in the man of the twentieth century, restless and distracted as he is, his respect for moral and intellectual values, we want to bring him back to thought and meditation, and to do so we propose to give him free drinks and free concerts, and possibly free dances as well! Libraries are sanctuaries of the mind where man can realize his true stature, and to attract him there we offer him a free cinema and God knows what—packets of cigarettes, sticks of shaving soap, tubes of toothpaste. If it is true that we have come to such a pass, then I say that the world is really in a bad way.

No, it will not do. The public must be made to realize that its dearest interests are at stake, that well-being, social justice, worldly delights, outward progress, all depend on the true use of the intellectual faculties, and that without books, which are the proved receptacles of knowledge, our individual and collective life is in danger of being submerged in a barbarism of which neither our children, nor our children's children, will see the end. Every man of goodwill in the community must realize that the cultivation of the things of the mind is an essential condition of a sober, righteous, and godly life, and that the book is the very symbol of religion. It is quite wrong to let the man in the street think that because he wants to buy a book he has the right to a seat at the circus, or an hour at the opera, or perhaps a boxing-match or a bull-fight. If the reader of today does not like reading for its own sake, then he had better give it up, and that will at least put an end to the present humiliating situation.

Big efforts such as book fairs, special book days, and the like, have their value, but anything that is liable to add to the present confusion of values, anything that may still further perplex our already perplexed minds, is suspect and should be disallowed.

I know that in some countries they think that spiritual causes, such as religion for example, can be furthered by fanfares and bazaars and sky-signs. That seems to me to be quite mad. You might as well fire off crackers to advertise silence, or preach solitude among the crowd and bustle of a fair.

Mind can only be helped by mind, and writing must save writing—the written word should be able to defend the cause of the written word. All who believe in the efficiency of a method which has stood the test of the ages, all who believe that books have raised us above the animals, all should unite, and it is not a moment too soon, in this crusade.

Advertising is not a very new arrival in the book trade—for some time before the War the wiles of advertising were beginning to offer temptations to publishers and authors. But it is only since the War that the methods of advertising have been deemed to be strictly applicable, and the phenomenon has developed rapidly; it may be said that the last fifteen years have sufficed to show definite results from the experiment. These results concern both authors, in their attitude to their craft, and publishers, in the economics of their business.

Before estimating the practical advantages of advertising I should say that, in the moral sphere, it has done harm to the cause of literature. That is why it is proper to examine it in cold blood, without any illusions. The act of literary creation is a spiritual one, and reading no less so; but between the acts of writing and reading there is room for a certain amount of commercial enterprise. The book is an article of commerce like everything else, like the cross, the pyx, or the wafer. "Everything's worth something," Thomas Pollok Nageoire once remarked heartily. It is possible to admit this state of affairs without making it too pointed. I have seen strange advertisements for communion wine which have shocked me deeply. "Everything's worth something"—yes, that is admitted, but certain negotiations should be discreet out of respect for the nature of their subject. Literary advertising, through the extravagance of its claims, has debased the cause of the book in the eyes of the whole world, and, what is more, has liberated all sorts of unworthy desires among authors.

In the first place it has developed a taste for surplus profits, artificial profits which really have nothing to do with artistic work. This is a most deplorable state of affairs. A wise and competent author cannot but be interested in the reactions of his readers; but how can he be aware of them if he allows all sorts of factors, which he cannot even control, to come between him and them? The essential thing for a writer, even one who is dependent on commercial success, is to know exactly how he affects his readers. Publicity has made it quite impossible for him to arrive at a true computation.

It has produced puerile rivalries among authors, and it has engendered among them a grasping attitude, which has certainly not raised them in the estimation of their publishers. The daily hope of seeing their names or their portraits in the newspapers must have been a torment to the simple-minded; and press publicity, which is a still more devastating affair, has first flattered and then wounded that childish pride which has always been part of the nature of literary men.

Not long ago, at a party in the provinces, I met a lady whose name is very well known because it has been associated for the last twenty-five years with a drink for which the publicity has been enormous. This lady spoke to me ingenuously of her husband, the distiller. She came to the subject of his publicity, smiled, and said with pride:

"My husband is so pleased!"

"I am sure he must be," I replied, "it brings him in a lot of money."

"It isn't only that," she went on; "the other day he came home from Paris simply beaming and said: "My name is all over the place. We are a success!"

Listening to this good lady's words I realized one of the most remarkable features of modern publicity; it succeeds in convincing its masters. The author who writes up his own copy, the enthusiastic paragraph, the dithyrambic blurb, is soon taken at his own valuation. He forgets that these ecstatic appreciations are the product of his own brain. As a result of blowing his own trumpet he no longer finds pleasure in the eulogies of others, and all outside criticism seems flat, even when it is favorable. He comes to the conclusion that he is not being properly rated; he loses his sense of self-criticism; everything seems to be small beer in comparison with the heady spirits which he has distilled himself, or which have been made to his specification in a commercial laboratory.

From the point of view of professional morality I should say that literary publicity has a fatal influence. Can we suppose that it makes up for the damage it does by virtue of its economic results? Are we justified in thinking that advertising, while debasing one aspect of literature, assists it from another point of view by tending to extend its empire? I must say I doubt it.

It is obvious at first sight that advertising methods have put over many books which would otherwise never have left their publishers' warehouses; they may also have increased the distribution of good books by speeding up the tempo of business. But what opinion has the public formed of these methods? An unfavorable one without a doubt. It is difficult to estimate the effects of a quack medicine, especially when it purports to fortify or purify the blood; but it is quite simple to arrive at the conclusion that, notwithstanding its special publicity, a particular book annoys, bores, or revolts us. The public, usually docile enough, knows very well when it is being exploited; it gets annoyed then, and its annoyance is extended to books of all sorts, good and bad. The economic crisis has aggravated this situation, for whereas it is no serious matter to buy a bad book when one can afford it, to throw money down the gutter when times are hard is maddening in the extreme. The reading public is getting restive. Already those authors who owe their reputation to advertising methods are falling into disrepute, and all the rest, though less affected, are suffering from the general discontent.

It might be said at the present moment that the preliminary experiments are finished. What are the results?

Showy, over-laudatory advertising is today condemned—only a few die-hards still believe in it. I cannot think that it pays for itself. For good books it may help a little though it can never make or mar them; for bad books, seeing that it is ineffective and costly, it is usually abandoned in the early stages by the publishers. Nearly all the reputable authors have ended by dispensing with the services of this alleged magician. Does that mean that literary advertising has lost the day?

Not at all. There are plenty of traces of insanity left.

In the old days the public used to go to the bookshops for information about new books; they took the first step. They may have been helped by the critics, for there was a time when criticism, even unfavorable criticism, was welcomed in the literary profession—I mean the sort of criticism that was not corrupted by publicity; when it is, the state of affairs is still more lamentable. Today the public expects to be told about everything at home, from the early morning onwards.

If, as may be hoped, literary advertising will confine its activities in future to simple announcements of new books, I realize that a limit may be set to the damage. Nevertheless, the book trade will have to reckon with increasing expenditure, and as for the prestige of literature, it will not emerge enhanced from the book racket.

X

ARE BOOKS MERCHANDISE?

I THINK I have emphasized that under present world conditions the book seems to me to be, if not the only instrument of culture, then certainly the most important one. Yet the book business is more mismanaged than any other; in France, at any rate, it is left to luck and routine, with occasional rash and ill-considered experiments.

The publisher's job is certainly a difficult one, but the publishers have done very little to see the problems of their profession clearly or to resolve them. Many of them take the view that the book business is like any other, and that the book is first and foremost an article of merchandise. I readily admit that the book trade, especially just recently, has had to face strong competition—I have already referred to this point at length—and I also admit that economic depression has aggravated the crisis, so that it is not a propitious moment to inaugurate investigations and reforms in publishing. Books in their social aspect raise numerous problems, some of which are purely psychological; and the conditions of success and failure, the influence of political phenomena, of seasonal variations, of custom, the life of the book in time and space, by which I mean the history

and geography of a given work or group of works—
these are some of the questions which in more prosper-
ous times would have deserved examination, and out of
which some sort of order in the book trade might have
been evolved. Books are living creatures, and their biology is yet to be discovered.

Do not let us think about these matters for the moment—the crisis is too serious. Let us rather consider a
few immediate reforms, and let us put forward some
proposals, always remembering that in the world of publishing there is at present no professional discipline.

Between the publisher and his public stands an indispensable middleman, the bookseller with his shop.

The bookselling business is not one of those that can
be tried without any special preparation. It is comparable to a profession in that it demands technical knowledge, some experience, methodical work, and a gift for
observation of human nature. A good bookseller, however commercial his business, is never without information about authors and their works, and he takes the
trouble to read and keep himself up to date. Like a
doctor or a lawyer he has to know his customers and
instruct himself in their various tastes, the delights of
Onesimus, the passions of Theodule, the misfortunes
of Bridget, and the opinions of Eusebius. A bookseller
who is worthy of his trade does not confine himself to
keeping an eye on his customers and selling them numbers of books at a profit, but plays a constructive part,
selling Claudel to one, recommending Giraudoux to
another, propagating Gide here, and grafting Mauriac
there. A bookseller who loves his trade will delight in
nice distinctions. With a book in his hand he will think:

"I believe 1 can get Smith to like that book. I may be wrong, but it's worth trying." He can play all the strings, even the most subtle. Once a bookseller said in my presence to one of his customers: "You don't like that book? That's extraordinary. Mr. Robinson doesn't like it either—which made me certain that you would. . . ."

I know such booksellers. They could, if they would, mold the spirit of a town, rouse it, give it direction.

It requires considerable capital to set up a bookshop, and the overhead expenses are heavy. A good bookshop must have a telephone nowadays, and it must have a complete outfit of reference books; it must also have a well-educated staff, qualified in a sense. There are some good bookshops in all our important provincial towns, and a great number in Paris. The life of these book-shops is an essential factor in the book problem, and, as I have said before, the problem of the book is the prob-lem of culture in general.

Yet the very existence of these bookshops is threat-ened today for a reason that is almost paradoxical, a reason that must be examined resolutely in cold blood.

Recently the publishers, hoping to further the cause of the book and indirectly their own commercial in-terests, made a big effort to increase the number of retailers. The argument seemed simple, but it is really simply silly: "The man in the street fails to buy books because he is not tempted to do so—because he has to hunt for them. Put them under his eyes, scatter books everywhere, and the public will want them."

The result is that the book trade has become a para-site among a host of other businesses. It used to happen

that the genuine bookseller, in order to meet his difficult situation, would sell leather goods and stationery;
but now it is the other way round; the book has come
to be an adjunct to other sorts of trading, and books
are to be found on sale at tobacconists, hairdressers, and
public-houses.

Is this a triumph? Far from it. This method may have
disposed of some books of no value, but it is highly
risky because it endangers the legitimate book trade.

I do not here criticize these small agencies; they are
given a big discount, they are encouraged to take up
books as an extra business without risk, and told that
they do not need any special knowledge; I even doubt
whether this additional business makes much profit for
them. But I have every reason to think that the established bookshops lose by this state of affairs, and this
constitutes a danger.

The keen reader who wants to buy a book does not
mind taking the trouble to visit his bookshop. But the
reader who is attracted through these small retail agencies is only a chance reader—he does not make a fortune
for the small shopkeeper, and he lessens the legitimate
profit of the real bookseller. This latter cannot very well
reduce either his overhead expenses or his staff, and he
will soon be playing the part of an honorary librarian—
people will come to ask his opinion when they want
information for nothing.

Need I add that this system of miscellaneous retail
distribution, far from helping the cause of the book,
tends to discredit it? The public is indifferent, and soon
becomes accustomed to seeing books mixed with pipes
and haberdashery, and the book, which is the vehicle of

all knowledge, gains nothing from such neighbors. The atmosphere of confusion is gaining ground.

It is estimated that in one of the quarters of Paris there is a bookshop of sorts to every two hundred and forty inhabitants, a proportion which is higher than in any of the other trades or businesses, including even the wine shops.

XI

LENDING LIBRARIES

WE cannot get far with the problem of the book without saying something about lending libraries.

They are the cause of a remarkable dispute which has not yet been settled, and which rages so hotly that we are apt to forget that the fate of the book at the present moment depends on much more serious factors; but seeing that this dispute brings up certain general considerations it ought to be examined, at any rate, in its main outlines.

The term "lending library" is applied to all those establishments of various sorts which lend magazines and books. The subscription is a variable quantity and may be in the form of a lump sum, or so much per volume for a specified period, or some other arrangement combining the two systems. The book is an article of commerce; apparently it belongs without question to the person who has bought it, and this person has at first sight an absolute proprietary right over it. He can destroy it, give it away, or lend it, ten, twenty, a hundred times, according to his whim. He can even, in the present state of the law, hire it out for money without referring to anyone, and can make theoretically unlimited profits out of this process.

Some authors are of the opinion that this liberty of ownership is in certain respects improper, and that if a book is used for profitable trading after its purchase, then it is only right that the authors should have a share in such profits.

In making this claim authors make the most of the example of the artists. It is generally known that some pictures, bought by amateurs for a definite price, have been sold, then repurchased, then sold again a great number of times by other amateurs, or by dealers, or by businesses acting on behalf of the galleries. The successive sellers have sometimes made big profits, and on each of these operations the State levies a tax. Other middlemen can intervene in the transactions; only the artist, the real creator, finds himself excluded from these profitable operations.

Now, as is also generally known, the artists and their lawyers have waged a successful campaign for their continuing interest.

Following their example the authors have embarked on a campaign for some similar sort of continuing interest in the works let out on hire from the lending libraries. Various literary associations have joined the dispute, but no definite solution has yet been offered.

The question is not a simple one. It presupposes very elaborate bookkeeping. But the interested parties urge that the recognition of rights of mechanical reproduction and performing rights has raised similar problems which have gradually been solved satisfactorily.

Let us hope that the authors' rights will prove to be assessable, and that this dispute will be settled to the satisfaction of the parties concerned.

Authors have some right, I admit, to a royalty, if only a very small one, on the takings of the lending libraries; but their main concern is to be read as much as possible. The author's interest is entirely bound up with that of culture in general, and the cause of culture is linked with the cause of the book. Any dispute which may do harm to the future of books in a practical way is to be avoided, or to be undertaken only with the greatest caution. Reading is dying out, at any rate among the big public, and will soon be replaced by other systems of information which have not yet passed the test of time, and from which I personally do not anticipate any very good results. If the conflict of the last few years between authors and lending libraries were to end in the suppression of the latter, with resulting diminution in the number of readers, then I should say that it would be an unqualified misfortune for culture and consequently a disaster for authors.

There are a certain number of organizations who lend books for nothing. No author in his right mind objects to this diffusion of his ideas; on the contrary, it is the constant hope of the writer who is worthy of the name that each of his books, which are the vehicles of his thought, shall be read by the greatest possible number of interested readers—readers who believe in him, who are, if you like, his disciples. What some people object to in the success of the lending libraries is the idea that literary property is thus falling, wholly or partially, into the public domain, and is making money, in the way that capital does, for a privileged minority of which the author is not one.

This apparent injustice is not a serious matter. The

real disaster would be if the public were to abandon reading altogether. Things are tending that way. We must not shrink from contemplating such a possibility, or from envisaging the effects it will have on the future of civilization.

The lending libraries offer certain advantages to the book-lover, which the public and free libraries cannot. They get the new books, usually several copies; they register their customers' wants and try to satisfy their individual needs; they are usually installed in book-shops. It often happens that the reader who likes a book he has borrowed will want to buy it, either for his own shelves or to give to one of his friends. Therefore I do not believe that the system of borrowing prevents the buying of books. It is even possible to argue that the lending library is a valuable ally of the bookshop, that it constitutes a sort of sample room. Moreover, I have noticed that the users of bookshops and libraries like to meet and discuss books either among themselves or with the staff of the shop. Thus literary clubs of a sort are formed in a town or in a district, where people can compare notes with others, handle the books, and form what I may call pre-judgments.

Taking it all round, I think that lending libraries are very necessary, and that they have cultural value. Now that the book is in danger they are precious fortresses. If a simple and practical system can be devised which will satisfy the other contestants I shall be pleased, but I think that the first necessity is to safeguard the lending libraries. Every time that a bookshop fails or a lending library closes its doors I say that in the present state of affairs it is a defeat for the spirit of man.

XII

INTELLECTUAL EXPORTS

FRANCE owes much of her moral prestige to what are termed her intellectual exports—works of art, plays, works of science, literature, and philosophy. These intellectual exports will soon be reduced to nothing, and as far as books are concerned, whether scientific or literary, the situation is as bad as it could be. The economic crisis which is affecting all trades is ruining the book business in France. Many countries can no longer buy our books because they cannot export the capital to pay for them. For example, in Germany, that omnivorous reader, the financial situation is such that the French publishers have given up business altogether rather than lose their investments in the form of stock. Austria and Hungary can hardly afford anything, and Russia is closed for more complex reasons. Other countries, such as Greece, Roumania, and Portugal, are in a state of flux, and Italy is for the moment in the grip of troubles which distract her from the exchange of intellectual ideas. South America buys next to nothing. Belgium, a nation of readers, is in distress, and since French is one of their two national languages the publishers have to make the best compromise they can. Generally speaking it can be said that French books, which once used to carry the message of our genius round the globe, will soon cease to go outside our own frontiers.

We are all involved in this misfortune. If our wines and our motor cars, our vegetables and our fruits, are to be left on our hands, it is surely a serious matter for our reputation and our finances; but if French ideas can no longer leave France I say that it is a disaster for us and for the whole world.

Alfred Vallette once said to me some years ago: "Do you realize that the complete poems of Jules Laforgue are out of print? We can't reprint them without losing money. But we're going to do them all the same. Laforgue is a minor master, of the symbolist school, and we must have him in our catalogue, even if it means a sacrifice." A week later, having thought it over like the good business man he is, he said to me: "We're going to reissue Laforgue, but in two volumes instead of one; in that way we shan't lose so heavily." At the rate things are going now we shall soon be at a stage when the publishers will no longer be in a position to lose money. What nearly happened to Jules Laforgue will be happening to the great masters. It is not extravagant to suppose that one day not very far off, failing a good enough sale, Descartes, Pascal, and Montaigne will be turned out of the bookshops and relegated to the dusty shelves of the public libraries, and soon after that—who can say?—to the archives. Those who are familiar with the condition of the book trade in France can no longer conceal their anxiety.

XIII

THE COST OF READING

NOTHING strikes the traveler in South America more than the sight of a people intoxicated with love for a culture which they seek with all their strength. As in a family where an heir is awaited who may be a redeemer, so everything is ready there for the birth of an autochthonous culture. Libraries are provided, and the schools and the institutes are magnificent. Poets are already beginning to make their appearance, some of them with success; the novelists are full of promise; and there is evidence that great painters will spring from the soul of this society. Historians and philosophers are at work. Latin America has already produced excellent works in every genre, which are not yet numerous enough to satisfy her vast appetite. She is now beginning to ask for assistance, to seek new lights, and she awaits a lead from our divided Europe, a Europe whom she condemns coldly, perhaps harshly, in political matters, but whom she still admires in the spiritual order.

In that part of the world France's reputation has long stood very high, so much so that South American readers who want to know something about English and German literature have to rely on inaccurate and badly written translations; whereas for communication with France, Latin America needs no intermediaries. We are read in our original texts, which is a great advantage. The word "influence" can easily be misunderstood. It is a damaging word, and I will not use it. In order to express the links between Latin America and France up to the present time we may use such words as "confidence," "friendship," and "communion." Shall we be able to use such words, such auspicious words, in the future? I doubt it.

French books today cost three or four times as much as they did before the War, and this is not excessive when one considers that in other trades prices have risen to five or ten times their pre-War figure. A book which sells with us at twelve or fifteen francs costs the Argentine reader, for example, the equivalent of twenty francs or more. But the Argentine peso has depreciated considerably since the crisis, and in the Argentine now the essentials of life are cheap. One can feed well for a peso, that is to say for about five francs. Thus the reader in the Argentine is offered material pleasures very cheap, and spiritual pleasures very dear. A French book for an Argentine buyer costs as much as four substantial meals—in the terms of simple barter it is worth two chickens and a half. So placed between Apollo and Mammon the reader is naturally tempted to make his offering to the latter. All the European countries have recognized this danger, and the German bookshops sell their works in the Argentine with twenty-five per cent rebate on the local price; in addition, they give their ordinary trade discounts on these prices, which must represent a considerable loss for them. The Italians in this competition are hardly less heroic; they sell their books at the local market price.

What is France doing? Nothing. Our books, as I have already said, are sold in the Argentine at from twenty to twenty-five per cent above the normal price. On the showing of the figures this rise in price is not unreasonable, for it has to cover the cost of shipping and of the return of unsold copies. But figures have nothing to do with such a problem. While other countries are thinking of founding their empires, France does not even take the trouble to keep her friends.

It goes without saying that the net result is humiliating for us. A few more years and France will have lost all her moral influence in a country which is obviously one of the countries of the future.

We can still avert this disaster—for it would be a disaster. Sacrifices must be made by the three interested parties. Who are they? I should say without hesitation the publishers, the shipping companies, and the Government.

I am aware that the responsibilities of publishers are heavy; moreover they vary from day to day and are unpredictable. All the same the publishers must give in rather than lose everything. If they cannot lower the price—and that is a debatable point—they must be more amenable in the acceptance of unsold copies and "returns." The publishers of scientific books are particularly intractable; but scientific books are dear, and one copy left on the hands of a bookseller at two hundred francs, for instance, eats up the profits from the sale of five ordinary books.

The shipping companies should not turn a deaf ear to

these warnings. Their interests are at stake, less directly, perhaps, but no less certainly. People from the Argentine come to France because they have read our books, because they admire France and our writers, because they speak our language. Once the Argentine readers have acquired a taste for Italian or German books they will go and spend their holidays in Italy or in Germany, and they will travel by Italian or German boats where they can understand the conversation. All these factors combine to create a serious situation. To meet it let us suggest that shipping companies should undertake the free return shipment of unsold copies.[1] The weight of a few parcels is nothing on a big boat, and this simple arrangement would very much ease the financial situation of the bookshops.

As for the Government, need we attempt to dictate what it should do? Is that intangible personality, the State, willing to consider the vital interests of France? If it is, then the question is simple enough. Let the Ministry of Posts and Telegraphs agree to a reduction of postage on books sent abroad, and the problem is lightened—is almost solved.

Here I am giving a warning. Will it be heard in the present tumult? I do not know; nevertheless, I raise my voice. It is no longer a question of stupid rivalry between hostile nationalisms; it is now a question of a great art treasure, knowledge itself, the very soul of that humanity of which the world is in need, and of which it may be deprived by the blind opposition of short-sighted business men.

[1] It appears that this suggestion is on the point of being accepted.

XIV

THE IMMORTALITY OF PRINT

The great difficulties under which culture is laboring in France, as everywhere else, are now beginning to have repercussions which will soon be apparent even to the least observant people.

Many creative minds are turning away from what I might call typographic expression. Some do so joyfully in the hope of creating a new art; these are the enthusiasts of the cinema, who are trying to think without words, to think in pictures, in lights and shadows. It seems probable that, despite the existence of the talking apparatus, words will be nothing more in the cinema of the future than a sort of condiment.

Other minds are turning, willingly or from necessity, towards the radio. I cannot believe that they are driven to it by any irresistible urge. The radio artist does not see his audience; he gets no stimulus from them except at the cost of an exhausting effort of the imagination; and his pay is mediocre—a point to which I shall refer later. Everything combines to make me think that the writer who turns to radio does so because he wants to try a new career, to find new outlets, to reach a new public, to supplement his income, and last, but not least, to satisfy his tormenting demon. Such a man, who is really concerned with the permanent, has to be content with the transient. Books, booklets, printed matter are all fragile delicate things, but among us mortal beings they stand for a measure of immortality. I should say that no author can lightly renounce his right to fix his work in print, and to leave behind him a record of his work and passion.

The radio has not broken away completely from the written word—under present conditions a manuscript is required. Thus the author still has to think in words, which means more work but is a very good thing—yes, a very good thing in our present state of disorder. I think I am right in saying that genuine authors who speak on the radio intend to publish their work afterwards, that is to say, to give it its normal destiny. A few can do it—a very few; the rest have to resign themselves to the fact that their thought will vanish forever with the vibration of the waves.

The impartial observer is forced to the conclusion that in the years to come many publishing houses will go out of business. The big reviews which still give opportunities for original work of all sorts are holding on only by economic and political expedients which have nothing to do with literature. The bookshops are in a bad way. The new conditions of employment propound problems that they are not in a position to solve.

The person who today is still referred to as an "author" knows that he will soon be only a "talker"; he will not disappear altogether—he will always be needed —and he will carry on in the new society, but he will find himself stripped of most of his old privileges.

State broadcasting, which is typical of the rest, must have unpublished work, because it must be able to offer its listeners brand-new words. There is something to be said for it because it considers manuscripts which would otherwise languish in bottom drawers. Broadcasting is omnivorous—it absorbs plays, stories, tales, news, essays, and poetry. Let authors beware; broadcasting, which is for them at present only a supplementary, or possibly a complementary, occupation, looks as if, at the rate things are going, it may become the principal means of expression in fifteen or twenty years' time. It is quite in the cards that before long most writers will have the greatest difficulty in getting their work published, and will have to be satisfied with speaking through a microphone. The writer will soon become a troubadour, as in the Middle Ages before the discovery of printing. It may even be supposed that they will give up writing altogether, and prepare material which is specially designed to be turned into sound— perhaps in the form of improvisation on themes.

What does it matter? some say. A new art is coming into being. The inventor of myths, the creator of ideas, the one-time writer, will adapt himself to circumstances and keep his place among the powers that be. Alas, it is to be feared that this place will gradually become more and more insignificant. It was with a real shock that I consulted the official pamphlets on broadcasting. Many writers work for the Government broadcasting, and most of them are well-known men of good reputation. They are subjected to all sorts of tests: they must be men of ideas, and they must be able to put their ideas clearly and to apply them to the work in hand, that is to say, to create a text. They must be mobile, because broadcasting cannot be done at home. Finally, they must have vocal powers, which need special training. The payment for this work is utterly inadequate. It is a gloomy thought that in France, the great country of culture, the monetary rewards of authorship are much less than in practically any other country; it is depressing to realize that men, from whom so much is asked—and primarily the sacrifice of leaving their work in embryo—should receive such a beggarly pittance.

Comedians are rather better treated, and they have a chance to repeat their performances. But the writer must give more than mere time and breath; he gives something of himself each time; he is the creator, the first principle. He should have preferential treatment.

This depreciation of the creator, who is the discoverer, the inventor of images and stories, the man who makes words and ideas live, of the author in a word, is not strictly speaking the will of society. When a poet is taken under somebody's wing, given little jobs, pushed back into the ranks of mediocrity, all the world loses; if the secret soul within him, constricted by hopeless conditions, ceases to watch, to fight, and to pray, then the rest of humanity is on the point of being thrown defenseless to the lions of ambition, and our society is likely to return to primitive barbarism.

To champion the author in these troubled times is to champion the cause of culture, that is to say, the cause of mankind as a whole. Public authorities must begin to pay attention to this problem, and writers must unite to show that they have realized the danger to their cause, which, since it is the cause of the word, may in that sense be identified with the cause of our human species.

PART II

OUR PROFESSIONAL OBLIGATIONS

I

MASTERS AND ORACLES

THE early autumn rains have begun; the dry summer is nearly over, and before it finally disappears it gives me a farewell smile which I find sorrowful, because I am myself sorrowful.

I have left my desk littered with a hundred letters, each of them asking something, some simple urgent question, and I have gone out into my parched garden. There I can walk alone over the brown grass, there I can breathe the new scents around me, the last roses of summer, there I can establish a little order and peace among confusion.

I have already consumed the greater part of my life. Day by day I move forward into a tangle of stifling, poisonous problems, which interlace like deadly parasites. I am neither tired nor hopeless. I am anxious, but that is because I want to do my best. I want to be able to find the right answers to the questions that are put to me. Some of the younger generation have told me of their distress of mind, and I do not want to fail them. All the same, the idea of a premature or casual or presumptuous answer fills me with horror.

I pace up and down alone, along the worn grass

path, weighing things up and comparing deeds, ideas, and words.

And suddenly a little scene comes back to my mind. It is a memory of my youth, of our youth. We were twenty-six or twenty-seven years old, Jules Romains and I, and we were having our first plays performed, both in the same season, at the Odéon under Antoine's management.

That day we were at some play or other at the Théâtre des Arts and during the interval we walked up and down, talking, in the narrow corridors lit by a gray afternoon light. Romains seized my arm and said:

"Look!"

A few paces away from us three men were engaged in friendly conversation. We recognized them at once, and my heart nearly missed a beat. They were Maurice Maeterlinck, Henri de Régnier, and Emile Verhaeren.

Romains spoke with charming enthusiasm, almost with pride in his voice.

"Over there," he said, "is certainly one spot in the world where there is a rich vein of humanity."

We stayed where we were, holding our breath a little.

"Shall we speak to them?" I asked.

"No," he answered, "don't let's bother them."

I agreed with him, although I knew Emile Verhaeren personally. He had been friendly to us from the beginning, and had already invited us to his little house in Saint-Cloud where he lived in winter.

I was then on the footing with Maeterlinck and Henri de Régnier for which I would have wished. Yes; I mean what I say. I neither wished nor dared to wish for any other. I dedicated my works affectionately to these masters. Perhaps I might get a short letter of acknowledgment, and my cup was full. Much later, after the War, having received many tributes from him and having encountered him twenty times without saying a word, I took the liberty of getting myself introduced to Henri de Régnier through Alfred Vallette, who published us both. Ever since then Henri de Régnier has been particularly friendly to me and I to him, and Maurice Maeterlinck, too, has written me letters which bear witness to his understanding and sympathy. Not until I met him by chance on a voyage did I emerge from my deferent reserve towards him.

I met Anatole France once, a year before he died, at the house of some friends who had asked us both to lunch. But for this accident I should never have known that the old man read and liked my own books. I have seen Barrès twice, on a literary jury of which we were both members; I have spoken to Bourget once in similar circumstances. Work on juries and committees has given me a chance to pay my respects to several of the grand old men of the preceding generation. I wrote a book about Claudel in 1912, a whole book, without making any efforts to meet the man himself—whether that was right or wrong I will not discuss now. If I had not met Valéry through our mutual friend, Luc Durtain, that excellent writer and clever doctor, who used to cauterize our throats as a matter of routine, I should have never known him until we met in Adrienne Monnier's bookshop, or perhaps much later in the War when we used to work together. I have written once to Jules Renard, on a literary point, but have never set foot inside his house. I have corresponded with

Gourmont but never met him, and it is only because
Descaves once made a generous gesture to me that I
have taken the liberty of going to see him. I have seen
Moréas once, without speaking a word to him. Gide is
an exception; I saw him for the first time more than
twenty years ago in a little room off the rue Visconti,
at the Union pour la vérité. He was reading a paper
on two or three poets, of whom I was one. In his charming voice he read several of my poems—it is a happy
memory for me.

There is no point in multiplying these examples.
What I am saying about our masters and our elders
could also apply to my friends and colleagues. I have
tried to respect their work and their leisure and not to
importune them. Will my reserve be mistaken for cold-
ness? I do not think so. But is such reserve to be generally recommended? I am not sure—that is a question
that I want to examine some day.

Are we to accept Mauriac's dictum that our generation has been a "generation without masters"? I hope
not. But we must first consider who our masters are
and try to remember what we hoped for from them.

The word generation is conveniently vague; actually
it makes me think of friends of my own age, and, of
course, of myself. It was almost a tradition in our youth
to begin a literary career by publishing some verse.
Poetry has the power of transcending human experience, and musicians and poets often bear fruit before
they are twenty. To sing it is not necessary to know the
world—indeed it may be better not to know it. But
the theater demands wider knowledge. And as for the
novel, that is a work of maturity; with a few notable

exceptions the real novel, strong and sustained, is not the work of an adolescent. Thus it is that our earliest books were books of poetry, and our first masters were poets. But among those whom we honored as our masters, and to whom we raised our hymns of praise, many were already dead. To me that did not seem to be important. Of course, we were glad to think that Claudel or Maeterlinck breathed the same air with us—that is roughly how I remember it at the time—but when we sought other evidences of their genius, the fact of contemporaneity did not enter into our considerations.

Alive or dead, young or old, our masters gave us a double lesson. Firstly, a lesson in the art of literature; their works were in our hands, sustaining us, and we gave them our enthusiastic admiration without renouncing our right to free criticism. This enthusiasm used to thrive by sharing. We used often to meet in the evenings when our work was done and indulge in feasts of reading aloud, followed sometimes by heated arguments. Then we began to correct these filial devotions by cooler judgments and academic standards. After Mallarmé, Rimbaud, and Claudel we fell back on Molière and Shakespeare—a harsh probation for young enthusiasm, but a valuable one, because we must learn the glory of the classics; we must rediscover them ten and twenty times in order to appreciate their true flavor of novelty, that is to say, of eternity.

In making the acquaintance of books we were apt to lose sight of the men themselves. For a long time Claudel seemed as far removed and almost as unreal as Buddha, and his personal friendship for me today has not quite obliterated this feeling. I was in no hurry to get to know him, perhaps because I was afraid that I might have to make difficult adjustments.

So we lived primarily in the works, though without being totally unaware of their authors. I have referred to a double lesson, and I should say that what we sought from our masters, apart from literary instruction, was a rule of artistic life. I repeat, artistic life, because scandalous stories seldom reached us, and all we wanted was to live a life that should be fine and noble.

Most of the symbolists, our respected colleagues of an earlier generation, lived in poverty—not all, of course, there were a few exceptions—and usually in obscurity as well. Many of them were unknown to the general public, hotly discussed by a small group of highbrows, and dismissed altogether by the academic world. They suffered even more than the romantics from the divorce between the middle classes and the creative artists which was characteristic of the nineteenth century. Whatever shocks the future might have in store, we were then determined to lead an honest life, proof against temptation, true to the ideal of a pure and scrupulous art.

What could we have asked in a practical way from men who were mostly working in the dark, printing their works at their own expense, submitting to the ridicule of the public and the disapproval of the schoolmen, men who knew nothing of the bitter delights of literary brotherhood? Nothing. Living and dead alike shared our admiration, and we asked only to live, we thanked them only for having lived. Occasionally we enlarged our pantheon; without disowning old allegiances we made new ones; for new ideas were in the air, and each day we discovered new heavens and new earths.

We asked from our masters precisely what they had already given us, what in fact had made us choose them for such honor. We asked the right to love them secretly, a right which is the least disputable, and the most modest, of all claims. Such is the love of the disciple, who in a sense creates the master.

And that is what I am thinking as I walk down my garden paths this autumn morning. A generation without masters? No; we have had our masters, the masters we deserved, masters whom twenty-five years later we salute with affection and gratitude, masters whom we writers of the present day, already middle-aged and graying, will always approach with deference.

I know that the world is changing, that during this last quarter of a century it has lost its balance and its sense of direction. Artistic problems, which used to be in the forefront of our concerns, are today overwhelmed by moral, social, and political problems. I understand that the young men of today, men of the age of our own sons and nephews or young brothers, are beginning to complain, and that they are reproaching their elders bitterly. I for one do not blame them. I propose to examine their complaints, and, as a prelude to this discussion, I think it is not superfluous to undertake an examination of our own consciences.

I have explained how we chose our masters, and what we expected from them—we who began our career at the beginning of this century.

That the young people of today seek their self-expres-

sion along lines quite different from ours does not surprise me, but when I hear that they complain I begin
to wonder; and if I have reason to think that they are
complaining of us, then I pause and say, Let us take
counsel together.

The discussion has already been opened by a contemporary of mine, François Mauriac, in an article
which made a stir recently. Among the many articles
which have gone to the making of this discussion I give
precedence to an essay published by Daniel-Rops in the
Correspondant under a significant title, "Le Procès des
maîtres." The author thought that he would be able to
call me as a witness in these proceedings; that was all
that was needed to allay my doubts and give me the
right and the duty to plead. Daniel-Rops has done his
work well, and his argument may be summarized as
follows: The men of thirty or thereabouts, who were
almost abandoned at school during the War, have not
subsequently, when taking up their career—whether it
be a career in general, or a literary career in particular
—encountered any writer who could play the part of a
"master" for them, or would even wish to play such
a part. Some of these young men, he argues, want no
master; the rest have dispensed with one as best they
can. Daniel-Rops has not taken into consideration
formal and technical influences. "A writer," he says,
"can only be a master if he propagates ideas, which
by their content or their form are likely to appeal to
young men."

I will not for the moment question this definition
of "master," which, put in that way, is at once attractive and arbitrary. I must first compare the picture

which Daniel-Rops paints of literary youth with the pictures I have drawn from my own experience.

During the last fifteen years I have corresponded with many young men. I should say that some of them have had the same ideas about their literary masters as the ones I have described in the preceding pages. Not that I disagree with Daniel-Rops—he is a staunch advocate of his generation. But he speaks for only a minority of the youth, certainly the strongest and most caustic minority. He does not, and would not know how to, speak in the name of all these young men, most of whom, as I have said, ask of their elders simply works, proofs of mastery, a pattern of artistic life, and perhaps sometimes a little personal friendship and warmth.

Let us leave these inarticulate ones, who are more numerous than one might imagine, and let us try to define another variety of the species, the sort of young people who want to make contact with their elders and to mix intimately in their society. Since the War I have, like many writers of my age, met and entertained great numbers of young men. Some of them have evinced only a simple curiosity, easily satisfied, and without much consequence. Others having been to see me have come back again. I have looked them in the face and said half seriously: "Come again as often as you like. One day, perhaps, you won't want to come to see me.... Yes, believe me, I know how things go. The curiosity of the young is insatiable, and must have constant changes of diet. If one day in the future you don't want to come, very well then, don't. I shall understand and would prefer you not to. And if some years later you need to see me again, have no sense of shame—simply come. If I am alive it will be to be at your disposal."

Usually it has turned out as I have prophesied. Some of them have gone away to return after various adventures; others have disappeared, perhaps for good; and several of these young men have stayed to become my friends—have told me of their struggles, explained their difficulties, proved themselves with me as witness. Sometimes they have asked for my help. What for? That is what I want to explain.

In days gone by the master, for either artists or craftsmen, was an expert in some branch of art or science, and could train novices by his own teaching or example. This definition of a master, which is the first that comes to my mind, is not likely to lead to errors of thought. Daniel-Rops in eliminating what he calls "technical influence" from the argument has only aggravated the problem; he adds to the dangerous confusion between master and rabbi, a confusion which I hope to dispel in the long run.

The master's first duty is to excel in his own art. There are many ways of excelling in an art, and that is why one master may be much sought after by some of the rising generation, and misunderstood, or perhaps despised, by others.

I know very well that literature cannot be demonstrated in practice like pottery or anatomy; it must be admitted, however, that technical considerations, or, if you like, the art and craft of literature, have not received much attention from the young writers.

On reflection this is not surprising. Some of the youth of today, surfeited by present world disorders, have taken refuge in a sort of passionate negation for their literary expression, and have plunged into fantastic de-spair. Such experiments are never in vain; we watch them with heartfelt pity—only a fool would laugh, only a fool would try to thwart them; and it would be cruel to foretell the absolute certainty of final victory for those laws which have hitherto governed language and literature, in France above all other countries. One thing is clear, and that is the uselessness of technical discussion or controversy with men whose ambition it is to overthrow technique, perhaps to destroy it for the time being.

Many of the young writers, cured of their revolu-tionary experiments or strengthened by opposition, have made a frontal attack on the traditional difficulties, and thus find themselves in a sense at the beginning of their career. Although they may well find fault with the education they received during the chaos of the war years, these young men lack neither knowledge or tal-ent. I would not say that all of them have an important message, but they have a gift for observation, facility, and versatility, and many other good and even brilliant qualities. That they have not taken the trouble to de-velop these gifts, or to draw on the experience of their elders, is not their own fault—nor indeed is it the fault of the older generation; we must blame the excesses of the book trade from 1920 to 1930.

Whereas formerly the one ambition of beginners was to find a publisher, nowadays the young men of the profession have succumbed to the dangerous tempta-tions of easy money, publicity, and spurious reputa-tions. What saint, hardened by mortifying the flesh, protected against the snares of the devil, could have

resisted such entreaties? If the youth of the literary profession must needs call someone to account, then it
should be the publishers.

Here let me say, in parenthesis, that Mauriac and
Rops might urge that they have put the discussion on
a much higher plane, and that the "accounts" called
for are not material ones; that may be so, but we must
take one step at a time.

Can the modern writers hope to perfect their art—
assuming, that is, that they feel the need of doing so—
when their writings are torn from their hands without
any critical reading or constructive criticism? During
these mad years we happened to admit to some of our
young friends that only so long ago as 1906 we always
used to pay out of our own pockets for the first impression of our books of verse; their smiles of astonishment and commiseration had to be seen to be believed.
One of the most brilliant of our young writers, whom
I once criticized for hasty writing, said: "You have no
idea how we are run after!" Another, one of the most
gifted of his generation, answered some of my criticisms
by explaining that in order to keep his contract he had
to write a book in three days. Another young man, who
had published nothing, presented himself at my office
with a rough, supercilious work that was hardly read-
able and said, when I gave him the names of several
possible publishers: "I'll go to the one who makes me
the best offer." I have heard hard-bitten men of twenty-
six say: "I must make six thousand francs a month,"
or "I am leaving X——, he doesn't give me enough
advertising," or again, "I can get published anywhere—
I have fifteen thousand readers on my side"; and when

I told some of them that the men of my generation all had some other profession so that they could be free to write, they laughed. Rightly enough, for the publishers were knocking at their doors, offering them monthly payments, printing their books without even taking the trouble to read them, and putting into effect all the machinery of high-powered advertising. Parents began to bring up their children for a literary career, a state of affairs which, if Gautier is to be believed, had not been seen since the days of Chapelain, author of *La Pucelle*. The literary agents, with nothing to lose, fought among themselves for the first novelists, who in their turn were easily led astray, and soon lost all sense of that mutual trust without which no joint work, no true collaboration, is possible.

Can we wonder that these young men have turned a deaf ear, throughout this unhappy period, to any exhortations, however impassioned, on the subject of literary technique, tradition, and morality?

The sort of religious ecstasy which we used to experience when confronted by a sheet of white paper, the sense of using a hallowed instrument with respect, of writing under the watchful eye of a hundred venerable masters, such feelings have no place in a society that is dazed by the tumult of the market-place, deafened by the bellowing of the auctioneer.

I have spent whole days with men of my own age, many of whom are well-known writers, in discussing texts and plots, in comparing style and subject-matter, in criticizing the scope and expedients of our art. I have had no such arguments with our younger colleagues. They have been thinking about other things. They have had to reply to the unreasonable demands of amateurs, to struggle against the caprices of fashion and the vacillations of publishers, and to fight among themselves like gladiators in the arena. The result is that they seldom ask us for constructive help, but merely plague us to intervene in their favor in the exhausting struggle in which they are engaged. We have never evaded this duty, though we must often have hurt one in order to please another.

There is no doubt that the younger generation has had great, and sometimes dangerous, practical opportunities, and even Daniel-Rops himself, that bitter critic, does not deny that they have had masters of technique at their disposal. But if we look at the problem from the spiritual rather than the material point of view, then the accusations of the young men begin to gain force and pathos.

It seemed to me from the first that the boys who looked for teachers among their elders just after the War had, generously enough, mistaken master for employer, or perhaps had confused their ideas of "master" with those of saint, or rather prophet and seer.

This brings me to a new discussion.

In the last paragraph of his excellent essay on the *Procès des Maîtres,* Daniel-Rops writes by way of conclusion: "We respect many of our elders, but we follow none blindly." At first I put in the margin a single phrase, "Just as well!" but on reflection this little remark by Daniel-Rops seems to deserve further commentary. It is obvious that in times of trouble young men feel the need of following someone "blindly," and this need is touching and understandable.

If I had had the chance, in my early youth, of mixing with those whom we used to regard as our masters, I might have summoned up the courage to ask their opinion about assonance or irregular meter; not because there were no more urgent questions, but because most of such urgent matters, whether political, social, or moral, were buried too deep in my heart for me to be able to confide in anyone. As it was, I extricated myself unaided, and not without suffering, from my first metaphysical crisis, the crisis of adolescence.

The world, on the eve of hardly distinguishable, hardly imaginable disasters, did not seem to me to be a simple affair, but I thought that I should have time to tackle my difficulties one by one, and get over them patiently; deprived since boyhood of the so-called light of religion, I had painfully to reconstruct a universe for myself.

1914 rudely shattered part of my edifice. I was thirty years old. I must admit that during this terrible time I felt the need of a spiritual master, and on two occasions I felt as if I had found a true leader and experienced the joy of confident obedience. For advice about certain important moral problems I would have had to resort to correspondence, which was out of the question. Besides, whom should I ask? Most of the distinguished men whom I thought of as my masters in literature seemed to be disconcerted by the turn things had taken, and had set their eyes on distant horizons of the imagination. I had to find a way out of my difficulties alone, and to work out a line of conduct, and I soon formed the opinion that, deprived as I was of religious authority with its various moral and political connotations, I had no one to count on but myself.

After the War I had occasion two or three times, in moods of despondency or curiosity, to interview celebrated men who, rightly or wrongly, were looked upon as oracles. They offered me ready-made axioms, and I took great care not to repeat the experience.

Moreover, I was by then a mature man. On the main questions that the world put to me I had an opinion, not a dogmatic opinion, but one which changed, and is still changing, partly because I change myself as I grow older, and partly because the world around me is continually changing.

About this time—I am speaking of the Armistice and the early years of peace—I realized that the roles were beginning to be reversed, and that I was being importuned by questions from the young men, in fact, that I was being looked upon as a budding master. I had just published a book written during the worst years of the War, and this book, written for my own alleviation, seemed to touch other hearts and kindred spirits.

I can still hear my friend C——, generous-hearted and broad-minded, saying, as he left a meeting of some of the students of the Thiers Foundation: "You have given us a morality; now you owe us a metaphysic."

This remark touched me more than I can say. I always had, and still have, a horror of incompetence. I used to smell it out from afar, and was continually on my guard against it.

An example here will help to explain my meaning. Although the personality of Barrès was unfamiliar and aloof, I respected and admired him as a writer. At the beginning of the War I had been in the habit of following the articles he wrote in an important Parisian paper, and one day I noticed with interest that Barrès's article was on the subject of hospital units of a new type—I was serving in one of them and we had just been sent to the Artois front. This article, which I read eagerly, contained many errors and rash guesses. I came to the conclusion that since Barrès could make mistakes about one of these few questions on which I was well informed, there was every chance that he would be wrong and misleading about everything else. Immediately all Barrès's journalism seemed to me to be valueless—a harsh judgment, I admit.

Imagine, then, my embarrassment when I realized that every day, and every minute of every day, I was going to be asked for opinions which I could not give, when I realized that I was going to be forced to speak about a host of subjects of which I knew nothing, and could know nothing. This embarrassment soon gave way in favor of a firm resolve.

Today I know by experience that the needs and desires of men are infinite. When a passer-by stops you in the street and asks you for a match, let him only speak to you and at the end of ten minutes he will be asking you for God. Everyone, whether they know it or not, wants law and order, discipline and direction; everyone wants to put on someone else's shoulders the difficulty of assessment and the responsibility of final decision; everyone dimly seeks God and the life eternal, even people who are ordinarily cynical, skeptical, and insensitive.

I give what I have, I say what I know; I am a writer in the prime of life. I have seen many men and many lands, and moreover I am a doctor, and in the course of my profession I have learned a lot about humanity. That is my domain—not a very small one, and I should be able to answer many questions; but many more still are the questions which I must leave unanswered, which every honest man must leave unanswered.

The great writers—Tolstoy is the most notable example—have, by virtue of their works, aroused unlimited confidence in the hearts of men. At once men have turned towards these masters, and have asked them every conceivable question, everything that we might ask from God. Almost without exception the masters have replied—that is what I blame them for.

Daniel-Rops is certainly right when he says that the true master is the man who "stirs up ideas"; but is it right to include among the masters a man who stirs up bad ideas? And taking into consideration the vastness of human suffering, is it even possible to give wise answers to the mass of questions about which most men keep silent?

I know that the temptation is great. Sometimes an answer flashes out a cry of anger, or of common sense, or of friendship, or of compassion. A young Protestant priest comes to see me, and shares some of his doubts, I mean his religious doubts. At the end he says, "Ought I to leave the Church?" "Oh," I answer, "since you ask me, you have left the Church already." It flashes out of my heart, impulsively, and it is a good enough answer on the surface. But the priest goes back to his parish; he will be there ten years later—and it will probably be the best thing for him and for everyone concerned.

Men must have their prophets and their Messiahs; they acclaim them and proclaim them unceasingly. Very well, let someone undeceive them; it is the duty of an honest man. I once heard of a young Hindu, who had been specially brought up to be a notability of some sort, and who signified, when the time came, that he would not take up his work. I conceived a great respect for this Messiah who resigned.

I have met Rabindranath Tagore several times in a very formal way, and I fully realize that the Orientals do not hold the moderate opinions that I have just expressed on this subject. They derive a security and an authority from their religious traditions such as we of the West could never know.

Prophets have their uses in history; all the same, I mistrust them, and I will not try to imitate them. The question that every disciple asks is, "What must I do?" This is a very touching phrase, and the man who utters it awaits a divine solution. The prophet cannot afford to hesitate; his reputation and many other things are at stake—the cause, the faith, mankind. . . . The prophet does not hesitate; he stretches forth his arm, strokes his beard, and pronounces. He settles the question. He invents or repeats a striking formula, some sibylline formula, perhaps, which the disciple will analyze later at his leisure. Little by little the habit grows on him and he settles everything. So much the worse for the disciple, and so much the worse for the prophet!

I do not want to play the prophet, and if, in order to be what Daniel-Rops calls a real master, I must speak like a prophet, then I shall never be a real master. I shall only be a writer among other writers.

But in my eyes the master is he who refers us to our own conscience, which is the sole judge in such matters.

It has been said that in the last years of the Empire the Romanovs suffered terribly because no one ever asked them for anything. I understand this sort of suffering. If the voices, which have addressed me for many years with affectionate confidence, were tomorrow to be silent, I should be very sorry; but if to keep the concert going I must play the prophet, well, then, let the voices be silent!

I have three sons of my own; when I contemplate these young men I need hardly say that I am concerned much more with their interests and their future than with my personal influence, my name, and my fame.

II

THE SPOILED CHILD

I DO not know whether the younger generation still enjoys reading Pierre Louys. I would like to know what they think about a little story called *L'Homme de Pourpre*. I discovered it twenty or thirty years ago, and I shall take good care not to express any opinion whatsoever about it. Works, like men, change as they grow older, and any opinion that is not refreshed and corrected by a recent reading, by an annual—I was going to say a weekly—reading, is irresponsible in my opinion. The plot of Pierre Louys's little work is as follows. A famous Greek painter—it is in ancient Greece—has acquired an intelligent slave. The artist, who is painting a Prometheus, takes his slave as a model and tortures him by burning his entrails so as to be able to depict the features of a suffering man with the maximum of exactitude. Hearing about this barbarity the people demand justice, and an angry mob assembles outside the windows of the studio. Then the artist appears and shows the crowd the finished picture; whereupon they are struck with enthusiasm, renounce their revenge, and utter cries of delight to celebrate the birth of an immortal work of art.

There is much to be said about the methods of this

realist painter. A hot iron does not produce the same effects as a vulture; besides, Prometheus' liver renewed itself continually, and this is an "experimental condition" that a scrupulous artist would have to reproduce. One could go on forever on the subject of this incompetent artist who had to inflict suffering in order to paint it. Let us leave it at that. That I remember this story, whereas ordinarily I forget novels and stories very quickly, is because it throws light on an obscure dispute that is constantly coming to life again, like Prometheus' liver, because it has something to say about the conflict between artists and society.

At the time when Pierre Louÿs published *L'Homme de Pourpre* I was a newcomer both to life and letters. Symbolism was our watchword, and I am not ashamed of it. In spite of the triumphs of the romantic movement and the supremacy of the great realists we had forcible experience of the popular antagonism to the creative mind. It was the time of poets accursed, of musicians martyred, of painters damned. The artists returned scorn with arrogance. Could they be expected to contemplate their past history with equanimity? For centuries, failing birth or fortune, they had lived in the pockets of the rich, eaten in the servants' hall of princes and dukes, begged their livelihood, danced attendance, presented petitions, picked up the crumbs that fell from their masters' table. Like Mozart, they had worn the red and gold uniform of the musicians of the household; like Molière, they had suffered the brutalities of a La Feuillade, bent the knee, like Goethe, to puffed-up masters, been jail-birds like Beaumarchais, swallowed keys like Gilbert. And then the face of the world had changed. The great were overthrown, the people learned to read, and a new sun seemed to be about to rise. Vain hope. The creative artists had to take up a new battle, to fight step by step against a flood of folly and ignorance, to make themselves heard above the tumult, offering their passionate works to the mockery of a crowd who, in Flaubert's words, could only think basely. The nineteenth century ended in uproar; the day was far from won; will it ever be? Will the artist ever reap a just and proper reward in a well-ordered and honorable society? Those are the very questions our parents used to argue about when we were children.

The superb indifference of romanticism colored thought right up to the beginning of this century and perhaps even till today. It is significant in the story of our progress that genius, mocked at, wounded, and suffering, has replied to its detractors by making exorbitant claims. Pride and ferocity developed in the literary coteries. They asserted that genius had a right to everything, that the end justified the means, that for the few chosen spirits, above the common run, every sacrifice should be made, apophthegms which would have astonished La Fontaine, Racine, John Sebastian Bach, or Nicolas Poussin, those great gentlemen of more serene ambition. This doctrine is still in favor today in some quarters. "The great creative artists," writes a biographer of Mozart, "need unlimited freedom, moral and material," a statement which makes one smile when one remembers the way of life of poor Wolfgang Amadeus.

It seems to me that the little story by Pierre Louys which I summarized above illustrates one page of our story very well. The artist is the gentleman of a new aristocracy. Are we forever going to refuse him recognition and discretionary power, seeing that in return he offers mankind the treasures of eternal beauty?

The coining of new ideas is a dangerous business. As our new idea spreads through the world it gets old, is gradually changed and degraded. It makes sober people smile—yet it goes on its way rejoicing.

All the middle-class folk who have survived old Flaubert's thunderbolts agree that the artist is a peculiar person. But in gaining admittance to so many good-natured hearts this idea has lost its romance. The artist is no longer a semi-divine being, mysterious, disturbing, the bearer of a sacred torch, a sort of priest or missionary, and frequenter of high places. Nowadays he is an "eccentric," a "freak," or a "character." He is not always condoned—we must be careful not to exaggerate—but he is allowed certain licenses and minor eccentricities, and he is referred to with a smile and a shrug of the shoulders. He is grudgingly allowed certain tiresome privileges, such as not paying his debts, forgetting his promises, and letting down his friends. In fact, he is a sort of spoiled child whose pranks are recounted with a nice mixture of surprise and malice, a spoiled child who may amuse himself by catching flies and tearing off their wings, and is scolded with a smile.

Alfred Vallette said to me not long ago: "For fifty years I have associated with novelists, poets, and artists. I have never had the least dispute with any of them. I realize that they cannot be judged by ordinary standards, and that one is bound to get annoyed if one attempts to hold them to the letter of the law. Many of them behave like children in business matters and like rogues in ordinary life. They are so unsophisticated that they would be surprised and hurt if one were to point out the error of their ways."

And Alfred Vallette added, smiling philosophically: "There are so many likeable fellows among them that no one really wants to quarrel with them."

This kindly sally filled me with shame on behalf of those to whom it refers. It brings the question of character into consideration.

Character, which often has nothing to do with ability, informs all genius. Character is rarer than genius, if we use the former in its absolute sense; indeed, character is the most enviable of all the gifts.

Vauvenargues has written somewhere the apparently clumsy phrase: "No man has had a share in all the gifts." I say "clumsy," because the idea of totality excludes the idea of sharing, and I suppose the phrase is laughable because, like all truisms, it is solemn and ingenuous. However, Vauvenargues makes the remark in connection with a great poet, and we pay attention for that reason.

For we want certain people to be endowed with all the gifts of the gods; not through love of such people, but by reason of our inordinate self-respect and our admiration for the human race. For a great artist to have every gift would crown our happiness.

Of all the gifts the one we ask for most fervently and insistently, on behalf of the artists we admire, is the gift of character.

I know men whom nature has treated lavishly, men of great creative energy, sensitive taste, a highly personal style; they may even have the external graces—good looks, a pleasant voice, a friendly handshake, and goodness knows what else. I would not ask for a glass of water from such people; I would not ask them to help a friend in need, to settle a dispute, to share a burden or to accept a responsibility—I would not even expect them to offer a helping hand or to take the slightest notice. They are virtuosi, tenors, acrobats (in safe jobs), performing dogs. I admire them, or rather I admire the sport of nature which has endowed them with their unique gifts. All the same I despise them a little, though if their gifts were to be withdrawn—such a thing might happen—these men would suddenly go out of fashion, as it were, and become less than a sucked orange, less than a crab-apple.

I know men who have what they call in artistic circles a strong personality. They are often incapable of making a decision, of settling a friendly dispute, of giving advice, of rendering the slightest service. I might go to them for amusement, and I rate them about equal with the best courtesans.

I have had enough experience of life to say with certainty that whereas I admire great artists I admire great characters still more. To them I offer my tribute.

But what is the good of talking like this when the near future is going to end all these disputes? Society is redistributing rank and wealth, and the time of the spoiled children, the fools, and the jesters is over. What part will the artists play when society is in the throes of political experiments?

III

OBVERSE OF SUCCESS

"Slavery and Infamy are the merited chastisements of success...." "A best-seller is the gilded tomb of a mediocre talent." These biting epigrams are to be found among the writings of Logan Pearsall Smith.

Logan Pearsall Smith is a discerning critic. He has published some little prose poems which Valéry Larbaud calls "poèmes à mi-voix," delightfully translated by Philippe Neel. I regret to see the author of *Trivia* making such rash aphorisms; he richly deserves the punishment of a thoroughgoing success.

The word "success" cannot be used casually nowadays. During the last thirty years, since the entry of commercial ambition into literary society, the word has begun to reverberate alarmingly. The demon of quantity, who will soon rule the world, is pressing home his attack and fortifying his positions in literary circles as everywhere else. I am sure that there are still some authors in existence for whom a letter from Gide or Claudel would spell complete success. Is it not success for a wise man to be read and enjoyed by his friends? To bring tears or dreams or laughter to such and such a person—that could be a real and satisfying reward for one who is not corrupted by success. But instead, artists and writers and poets, no longer content with their own natural success, the success that is proper to their style, must pursue success in an absolute sense, the only success that counts—because it counts in figures.

Yet the intervention of the quantitative demon appears to complicate problems rather than to simplify them further. What meaning can a standard of measure have as applied to the indeterminate or the indefinite? Where does success begin? How is it to be recognized? Where should it end? Or should it end at all? Tom's five thousand copies, of which he is very proud, make a very modest showing in comparison with Dick's fifty thousand. And Dick's fifty thousand, though a notable array, look paltry in comparison with Harry's three hundred thousand. And Harry himself shrinks to insignificance when compared with the huge best-sellers of Germany and England. Love and admiration are drowned in these astronomical figures. Compared with Jupiter, the earth is a small apple, and Jupiter is a poor thing in the presence of his master the sun, and the sun itself is a featherweight among those hundreds of stars of which the chief fact we know is that they are not the largest in this disconcerting universe.

Figures, which really gauge nothing, succeed in distorting everything. They make some strong and steady heads reel. Authors who apparently have all they need in the way of discriminating approval dream—not always in private—of a "public" success. Only, of course, "out of curiosity," and to see "how it feels"; just to fill their cup of satisfaction and to experience for once certain crude and powerful sensations. And since an

infallible recipe for "public" success is yet to be discovered this curiosity results in some nasty shocks.

Young men, spurred on by commercial offers, dazed
by big competitions and a sort of prize-hunting fever,
regard "quantitative" success as a preliminary step to
a career, as a sort of entrance examination. Henceforward, the game of literature will be played with the
whole world as witness, a world which cares nothing
for works, but wants only to see sport—winners, losers,
records, and casualties.

The spectator who looks at these antics with a seeing
eye is filled with disgust. If he is of a proud disposition,
if his views on art are lofty and uncompromising, then
he refuses to endorse the opinion of the majority and
he takes no notice of success.

This leads to inner conflicts and difficulties, and the
man who is dearly attached to work of high quality
strongly resents public apathy. Unless he is a selfish
hedonist he tries to make converts; but as soon as he
has made them he suffers because he finds them unworthy, or perhaps simply indiscreet or impertinent.
He bitterly regrets his former solitude, and soon turns
against the object of his affection. When Maeterlinck
first became famous his earliest supporters would have
nothing to do with him, calling him spitefully a "maga-
zine philosopher." I know men who genuinely respect
Claudel more because he has never had any academic
distinction, but begin to have doubts when they reflect
that their poet may be only one of the lesser stars—
an uncomfortable thought. Some people take the childish view that Giraudoux is no longer so enjoyable now
that his plays have become popular. When André Mal-

raux drinks the last drop of official literary fame—he
does not seem likely to refuse it—his name will be on
every lip, and his books in every library; yet those very
people who would have most wished it so will probably
be sorry. So does love tremble in the balance. These
people will agree with Logan Pearsall Smith when he
says that "a best-seller is the gilded tomb of a mediocre
talent." In my opinion they will be wrong.

They will be wrong to attempt to simplify, for their
own ends, a problem which history has shown to be so
complicated. Second-rate talent—Corneille, Racine, and
Molière, for example? What is the meaning of this spite?
Are we, through over-refinement of taste and excess of
scruple, to throw civilization to the winds, desert our
cause, and betray the art that we claim to serve? The
dispute is not of today alone; after the success of *Horace,*
which threatened to earn "six months' bread-and-butter
for the actors," poor Chapelain wrote to Guez de Balzac: "Such are the tricks of these mercenary poets, and
such is the fate of these venal plays!" Shade of Corneille!
A mercenary poet—have mercy on us!

It would be too easy to say that Pradon always got
the better of Racine. Fortunately for the golden age
Racine had the last word. Apparently he has it still.

Is Molière a mediocrity because they applauded the
Précieuses for four months on end, and because
L'Avare, on its revival, ran for a year? Let us steer
clear of such notions—they can be damaging. In order
to avenge the success of fools and knaves shall we deny
our masters their success which should be our own
consolation and guiding light?

Sainte-Beuve said that "the success of *Atala* was prodigious"; that does not diminish Chateaubriand in my eyes. Critics united in saying that *Werther* had an immense success; that does not lessen my respect for Goethe. I rejoice over present-day successes even more than past; Hardy, Conrad, Selma Lagerlöf, Gorky, Pirandello, Paul Valéry, André Gide, Colette—I choose widely differing types deliberately—the success of such writers, whose first flights we watched and were proud to see, this success, if we love literature and have faith in our art, is a personal success for ourselves, and a basis for new hope and legitimate pride.

All the same, if one of my sons were to decide to try his luck as a writer, and were to ask my counsel—in moments of enthusiasm I can imagine such a thing happening—I should give him only one piece of advice: "Beware of success."

And in saying this I should think first of success in our time, what I am tempted to call "American success," that monstrous phenomenon, brutal and unbridled as an assassination, which seizes a man, uproots him and tears him to pieces, then lets him fall to earth again, three-quarters dead, to rot and perish in obscurity.

And I should think too, in whispering my advice, of that other form of success, insidious, reasonable, wheedling, the success which gradually changes a man's course, which clips his wings and blunts his nails, and gently edges him into the slippers of fame; I should think of that success whose poisonous caresses sap a man's courage and drain his vitality.

Beware of success! Every success is a door closed behind you, a hope realized, a future pledged; every success is a renunciation.

Yes, beware of the sly attack of success. Scorn it. But how properly to scorn it when you have not achieved it?

Success is a searching test—we must not fear the test, nor must we claim it as a right.

If you desire success do not let your desire carry you off your feet; if you scorn it, let your scorn bear no grudge.

Some are strong enough to discipline themselves in everything—and can achieve control even over their success.

There are some good souls, men of genius perhaps, whom one glimpse of success will throw into ecstasy—then into the gutter.

There are other souls, turned in on themselves by nature, whom success may suddenly release to light and freedom.

I know many others who are blinded or intoxicated by success.

So, let us open our two hands, let us grasp the white ball of success in one hand and the black ball of failure in the other, and let us try to walk straight, keeping our balance.

And just remember one phrase: "Beware of success." The rest I have not explained—I am keeping it to **myself.**

IV

THE REVELATION OF GENIUS

JUST watch that boy, that young man, walking alone along the Paris pavement, watch him and follow him like a guardian angel through the crowded traffic.

He is still a boy, probably at school. He is a mental forager of anything that may happen to attract or amuse him, a secret drinker—of intoxicating books. He is proud and shy, and easily wounded. When he feels that he is being observed he keeps a stiff upper lip, but as soon as he thinks he is alone you will see him plunged into some dark despair. He is humbly dressed, and quickly startled; all the same, his eyes speak only of revenge, of power and glory. He smiles, for he is tender-hearted, then rapidly pulls himself together and plunges once again into the bitterness of revolt.

Follow this boy, follow in his footsteps, then suddenly, like the dark angel, seize him, ravish him, carry him off to the top of the high mountain and offer him the treasures of the world.

It is an unfair test. The idea of the treasures of the world is enough to shake even men who are practiced in self-denial. To renounce women—yes, I put women first—to refuse the countries of the earth with their

changing landscapes and their produce and their machinery and their toys, to renounce the land and the
cities, the forests and the flowers, to reject the respectful
salutations of the weak, the dignity of solitude, and the
elation of society, to be able to renounce all that pre-
sumes a soul tempered by the constant contemplation
of death, or by a desire vaster and still more consuming
than the promises of the devil.

Yet the boy hesitates. He gasps with distress. And
then, suddenly, he overcomes the temptation and shakes
his head vigorously. He renounces. He has made his
choice.

"No," whispers a voice that betrays alternately pride
and shame, "no, that's not what I want. I want simply
... genius."

The boy is not aware that genius carries all these
temporal blandishments in its train, or even that it is
capable of accepting substantial rewards. His idea of
genius, I am sure, is genius unadorned and unheralded,
a Schubert or a Rimbaud, a Villon or a Van Gogh, a
Baudelaire or a Shelley. Genius with a spice of disrepute, of suffering and martyrdom and sacrifice. Better
Schiller's cough than Goethe's good health, better
Beethoven's stuffy cellar than Wagner's royal radiance,
better Chatterton poisoned than Hugo in honored old
age, rather Chénier on the scaffold than Rubens
wreathed with laurels. But wait a moment. What this
boy asks, in exchange for all he has renounced, is not
a genius, or *his* genius, or a man of genius, but genius
naked and unashamed, the creative gift itself which
comes from God.

This young man, this boy, who would renounce the pleasures of the world for a star in the east, is to be seen daily in our streets and in our houses; I recognize him and I salute him secretly, for the sight of him fills me with affection and anxiety.

What does he know of this "genius," which he already loves more than life itself? He has but breathed the wind, heard the echo of its passing. He has not yet heard the true ring of the great works. He cannot measure the depths of the abyss which the great spirits have plumbed. Of all the major realities of the mind he draws for himself pictures that are alive, but distorted—or so it seems to us. But he has the inner experience of genius and that is worth any amount of rationalization; he has what belongs to the youth of the spirit, an instinct for genius and aspiration and transcendence of self.

If only this intangible flame can be grasped and imprisoned in the flesh, injected like a miraculous seed into this mortal clay, then the victory is won and the way to Olympus is open.

And so the struggle begins. But is it really a struggle? The boy plays in turn the parts of lion-tamer, suppliant, and bird-charmer. Sometimes he waits patiently for his dream, sometimes he prays on bended knee for the visitation, sometimes he runs round like one possessed, leaving no stone unturned, forcing every door, exploring every avenue. "Genius was here this morning. It appeared to me in my sleep. It flashed across my sky like a comet. It whispered in my ear while I was on my way to meet my best friend. It made me laugh in my employer's face, came like a flame between me and my love, walked before me in the street in the half-light. . . ."

The boy is exasperated by these tricks. Considering that he has made his choice, why cannot genius come without keeping him waiting? Why cannot it descend from the blue, complete and perfect? People talk about discipline and method and hard work. That's all very well, but what I want is a consuming flame. They say that Mozart studied under his father and twenty other masters, they say that Rodin chafed at the bit for years, Balzac spilled gallons of ink before he discovered Balzac; yes, but that's not what I want—I want the sudden flash of illumination, the perfect inspiration—it will come, and I shall win it by courtship or by conquest.

The boy clenches his fists and knits his brows in the struggle. He wonders angrily if there is no way of compelling genius. He achieves moments of blessed inspiration; then he tries to recapture the circumstances under which he has received these intimations of genius, the highest points in his life.

Such ardor deserves enlightenment.

The extraordinary thing about youth's subjective certainty of genius is that it goes hand in hand with a sense of irresponsibility. Whereas the mature creative artist usually regards himself merely as the agent of his work, the young man thinks that he is the primary source. He feels himself to be a privileged person, exempted from the necessity of estimating his own weakness or admitting his own artlessness. Inexperience does not trouble him because he is only the interpreter of his own mind, and he feels genius working in him like a divine ferment.

These ideas, the more surprising for being unsought, come to the young man during his periods of aridity and dazzle him, especially when he is tired at the end of some long and exasperating vigil, at dawn after a sleepless night, at the extreme limit of physical and mental strain.

The poisons of fatigue can soon upset the delicate mechanism of the mind. Just as an over-tired heart resorts to excessive and irregular palpitations, so the brain, in its fight against exhaustion and sleep, manufactures all sorts of monstrous and extravagant ideas unco-ordinated among themselves, and these ideas, by their very disorder and immoderacy, seem to their creator to have the true bearing and accent of genius.

Sometimes, too, the excessive nervous tension and the suffering of passion tear from the most secret fibers the strongest responses. The young man feels all that. While he is waiting distractedly he argues to himself that the poisonous drugs of fatigue are not the only ones, that there are stronger, more deadly, agents from which his frozen spirit might, perhaps, squeeze a drop of the divine elixir, drugs which may scorch him, rack him, push him to the very edge of the precipice at the risk of death. "Tobacco is a diversion, alcohol is a vulgar spur; but there is opium, there are ether, morphia, and their magic sisters. Men talk of danger—they draw lurid pictures. Ah well, it cannot be helped! Life itself, this dear and precious life, for one hour of true genius!"

Let me tell the story of my last interview with the poet Valère B——, who is now a shade among the shades of the departed. He came to us from the other end of Europe. He was a man of wide culture and sensitive mind. He came to Paris and invited me and some friends of mine to go and see him at his hotel. As we were leaving after midnight, Valère B—— took my arm. "Let them go," he said, "and come with me." He took me into his room, opened a drawer, and took out a syringe and a bottle, which he held up in despair. His voice was low, terribly changed, and he sobbed: "The bottle is empty. No more morphia, and the night is only just beginning. You are a doctor, M. Duhamel; write me a prescription; I implore you." And while I listened, mute with horror, this man, ordinarily so proud, went on: "Write, or I shall go down on my knees, I shall throw myself at your feet on the carpet."

Closing my eyes I can see T——, poet and philosopher of an artificial Eden. His face used to cloud over suddenly without apparent reason, and he would look at everything with a lost, staring eye, like a fish that has been caught. Then he would break off the conversation violently and escape to his dreadful delights. And I can see J——, clutching a bottle of ether in one hand and calmly holding his fountain-pen in the other. I can see M——, with his fine features, that crystal-clear soul, who was found one day stiff and cold in the hollow of his bed. I see B——, another poet, who had to spend his time thinking not about the vagaries of genius but only about how to evade his keepers, how to escape by the windows, how to get drugs by threats. I can see them all, all these unfortunate men who had not genius, but only a love of genius, a desperate desire for genius; and I see, too, the lurching crowd of drunkards who vomit against the walls of the town, evoking the names of

Villon, Verlaine, and goodness knows whom else. Musset, perhaps?

No, friends, genius is not the fruit of chance, nor of riotous living, nor of drug-taking. That would be too easy, and incidentally too stupid and too disgusting. There is no chemical or biological formula for the condition of inspiration or for the manufacture of masterpieces. Great men, overtaken by some terrible misfortune, have spent their whole life in fighting against the evil. They have saved their genius from poison and drugs; they did not *owe* it to them.

I cannot go so far as to say that genius is a healthy state, but I know very well that it always represents a victory over the powers of dissolution and death.

I write these words not to frighten my young colleagues, but to express my own inner certainty. Opium, morphia, ether, even alcohol, have the power of giving thousands of misguided people the idea that they have genius; but these poisons have not endowed the world with a single masterpiece. Let no one quote Baudelaire and *Les Paradis*—when Baudelaire is at his best his brain is cold and his insight cruelly clear. Let no one quote Verlaine—only the products of his abstinence are perfect, and it was on clear prison water that he wrote his most convincing works.

I know how bright the illusions of drunkenness are, but what is left of them for the awakening? Charles Nicolle, the doctor, told me this story. On one occasion he induced one of his friends who smoked hashish, and who claimed to write sublime poems under the influence of the drug, to write down his actual inspiration during intoxication; the only result was this very tame "hai'kai":

> Dans le cerveau d'un haschisché
> Un petit oiseau desséché
> Casse du menu bois.

I am fond of wine and I drink it; it is a wonderful gift of nature. I well understand that it should be used for the blood of the sacrament. But to find his true style the artist must wait until the last fumes of alcohol are dispersed on the breeze and his eye is clear again. If there is to be intoxication it must not come from outside.

As for the neuroses, is it not enough to have experienced their blight? Is there any need to court them? I was once told that a poet of undoubted talent who had just contracted a dreaded illness jumped for joy when the diagnosis was confirmed and cried: "Now I shall have genius!" That is the cry of a fevered imagination. The pox does not necessarily preclude genius, but it does not confer it—it is more likely to stifle it.

Maupassant, in the grip of disease, lays down his pen and is silent; he knows that his genius is dead. And what about *Le Horla?* someone will ask. It is now known that that masterpiece was written in 1887, and is not the product of delirium; Maupassant wrote it when he was in full vigor, in the middle of his creative life, as Léon Hennique pointed out.

Flaubert and Dostoevsky lived in terror of epilepsy; they certainly did not cultivate it. During the best creative period of his life Flaubert had no attacks and seemed to be completely cured—I take my information from Dumesnil, a sound doctor and great man of letters.

It takes time to write masterpieces and the period of exaltation of general paralysis of the insane is, after all, only short. Nietzsche worked in spite of, and not because of, his malady. One day the sickness triumphed; then eleven years of ghastly silence, of a living burial. And all that can be said about drugs and disease might also be applied to the passions which are supposed to be so effective in molding genius. Great men suffer terribly under real passion, but they do not solicit it; they bear their burden, day by day crying with a loud voice, "Eli, eli, lama sabachthani!" Only a wretched schoolboy would be deceived into thinking that he could draw illumination from great suffering by acting it.

Romanticism no longer gives us our masterpieces, and it still impairs our judgment. Young men, fling open your windows, and drive the phantoms away!

V

IMAGINARY MODELS

"WHAT! some twopenny-halfpenny little playwright has had the audacity to put a man like me on the stage! I shall lodge a complaint in the interests of good order— it is a positive duty to put down the insolence of such people; they are the pests of society; they notice everything so as to poke fun at everything." These were the words of a worthy Paris citizen who imagined that he recognized himself in the *Cocu imaginaire*. Grimarest, who tells the story, adds that some kind soul succeeded in calming him down at last by pointing out that he was not an "imaginary," but an actual *cocu*.

Molière did not always come off so lightly, and had some nasty disputes with his alleged models. Seeing that similar cases have been tried hundreds of times since then, one would like to think that the writer's position is appreciated today, and that although he may draw bitter reproaches on his head he will have little to fear from enlightened magistrates.

Unfortunately, it seems that there is no hurry to bury the hatchet. Recent news from Belgium has made me uneasy. Pierre Hubermont, a vigorous novelist, published not long ago a good story, called playfully *Hardi! Montarchin*. It is a picture of an electoral contest in a little provincial town; no bile, no venom, but plenty of fun; a frank sort of picture with the colors laid on thick. In fact, one of those books that are likeable because they are warm and living and smack of the soil. Much to his surprise the novelist found himself in the law courts. Five people claimed to recognize themselves in the book. The Hainaut judges, over-persuaded by local agitation, ordered the author to pay the plaintiffs the exorbitant sum of 21,000 francs. The case went to appeal, and the Brabant judges gave their decision—supporting, unfortunately, their colleagues of Hainaut. The rest of us look on and are deeply worried and, indeed, indignant.

For such an injustice is everyone's affair. It may be our turn next, like Hubermont and so many others, to defend our work against the rancor of bigots and maniacs, to go to the courts to plead for our own creations, the children of our suffering and our meditation. We may be forced to abjure the very principles of an art whose life-blood is truth.

The glory of French literature lies in the fact that it has taken real life as its model. Not that our great writers have lacked imagination or invention; but their best works are full of actual life—their own life or that of others. I have mentioned Molière, and, of course, I should have to name Racine and La Bruyère and Beaumarchais and Voltaire and Diderot and Jean-Jacques Rousseau; and Stendhal and Mérimée, and the Flaubert of *Bovary* and *L'Éducation*. I should have to mention all the masters—no, not all, because romanticism has led some of them away from the broad daylight. I could not find examples in Hernani or Ruy Blas or Quasimodo—those dream-creations are already disappearing in smoke, lacking the flesh and blood of common humanity. With Zola, confirmed romantic, it is easy enough to see where the artificial recipe takes the place of real knowledge. It has been said that Balzac was so harassed that he had no time to observe the characters he put on his stage. But why talk of observing? Balzac is a contemplative; he had no need to run after the world, for the world came to him. Balzac discovered the world within himself. Nothing can be created from nothing, and works which emerge from nothing can only amuse us for a moment, and then, lacking substance, return to the nothing whence they sprang. So Balzac had no models? Why, his models are with us yet, and we meet them every day of our lives. But because Balzac was so powerful a creator he has reshaped his models, with the result that they have unconsciously copied their own portraits, and are now living exactly in the way that Balzac laid down for them.

For each of his characters the good novelist has not one but twenty or a hundred models. He is himself his most versatile model and can serve for giant or dwarf; he samples all the potions himself, puts on all the costumes, tries on all the wigs. Line by line he asks questions and answers them, loves and hates himself, attacks and defends himself.

But while this moving drama is going on, this debate between the soul and its mirrors, what of our poor little village politicians with their local scandals, their family squabbles, their deadly hatreds and prejudices? We are trying to depict man, to know and understand him in all his aspects, and if possible to help him and enlighten him in the adventure of life—it is not a question of making fun of humble people or working off some idiotic little spite against them.

I am well aware that there are professional pamphleteers who promulgate scandal. These people have nothing to do with literature; no doubt one would fulfill their dearest hopes by bringing them to justice, and thus giving their baseness the reward of publicity.

But the artist, the painter of men and manners, has the paramount duty of testifying to his epoch. His task is difficult enough without our trying to make it worse for him.

Let the learned judges of Brabant, and of Hainaut, and of the rest of the world take notice; the true novelist does not draw pictures of Naomi, Anastasius, or Matthew with the absurd idea of upsetting those good people; he sees far beyond Matthew and Naomi, for he is making his contribution to the story of mankind. He may take a feature from one, a phrase from another, in fulfilling his duty as a witness, his function of busy bee, but do not ask him to reconstruct the world if you will not allow him to describe what he sees. Do not blame him for seeing clearly and hearing truly—he should be reproached only for bad sight or faulty hearing; and if he uses a sharp scalpel to open an abscess—well, it is because there are times when mere good advice is not enough.

As soon as an object has caught the novelist's eye it begins to undergo changes in his mind. It is amalgamated with other objects, it ferments, and is digested. It is submitted to a process of amplification and purification. The final result is so far away from the model that it can really be said to have escaped from it. The models are necessary, but they are always superseded, and anyone who recognizes himself in the author's work is merely presumptuous. I have a long personal experience of these matters and I can say categorically that the people who have been the sources of a writer's inspiration hardly ever recognize themselves, whereas people who have never been thought of are only too glad to identify themselves—a fact which makes this discussion a trifle ludicrous. If all the people who imagine they have discovered part of their personality in Salavin were to proceed against me I should spend the rest of my days in prison.

I realize that the law must respond to the claims made on it, but its highest function is to placate and remove difficulties, and to resolve conflicts without resorting to penal sanctions. All judgments of this sort are subsequently reversed by posterity with an ironic smile.

I do not think that man-made justice can understand and settle everything. If it could it would lose its prestige and its power; because it would be called in—such is the way of the world—to supervise the behavior of doctors and specialists whom the public have hitherto accepted as experts. It would be impossible to overestimate the dangers of such interference, which would paralyze action, enslave knowledge, and ultimately act against the best interests of the community. Artists and writers would have to consult a lawyer before they took up paint-brush or pen, weigh up the legal position and forearm themselves against possible, or rather inevitable, litigants; for even words of peace and love can carry insults to some ears. Surely such slavery is incompatible with the very essence of art.

The magistrates have hitherto been considered inviolable in the exercise of their functions. Inviolable, but not infallible. Their mistakes, though they may not be punished, may be recognized. If their unique position inclines them to mercy they will earn our gratitude. In wielding the mighty sword of justice they should not show less consideration and charity than they demand from us when we take up our pen.

VI

LOVE OF PROFESSION

EVERY autumn I give myself the pleasure of attending one of the sessions of the annual surgeons' congress. I no longer believe in what is commonly called committee work because real work of the mind seems to me to be incompatible with group activity. Therefore I use the neutral word "session." Like all affairs of its kind the surgeons' congress includes an evening entertainment, usually a dance. Sometimes I go to it, not without pleasure, to meet old friends and comrades. I mix with the crowd. There is very little dancing but plenty of talking. I listen because I am interested, and this is the sort of thing I hear: "You know, old man, the temperature went up to 102 in the evening so I decided to operate...." "I get quite good results by draining the wound...." "You are wrong in condemning radium...." "...As soon as I made the incision I found the stomach full of muck...." "...Yes, I know, mixed microbes are dangerous...." "It's convenient, but it's anti-surgical...."

These are deservedly distinguished men and not merely "artisans in human flesh." I know them. I know that many a one of them has a fine library, a collection of pictures, a taste for music and travel. There are some among them whom I could name as having encyclopedic knowledge. But all these men love their profession; and so, as soon as they have a chance to be together, among themselves, they talk shop, as the good craftsmen used to say; they talk shop and they enjoy it. They compare notes, share their successes, admit their failures, and argue keenly about their technique, their preferences, their theories, and their hopes. This love of profession is not peculiar to surgeons—physicians also have it and give similar evidence of it. I always remember gratefully a visit I paid some year ago to a patient who was in the charge of Dr. Fournier at the Cochin Hospital. The good doctor, when I had paid my respects, took me by the shoulders with that half-paternal, half-brotherly familiarity which his friends will never forget, and led me into the wards. "You want to know how things are getting on?" he asked. "You want to know why we are all looking so pleased? It is because we have found a new cure!" And how simply he spoke this admirable phrase!

Whether you are at a political congress—fortunately that does not often happen to me—or at a family gathering, or on one of those organized cruises, you will soon see the doctors getting together in a bunch, even when they have divergent ideas and interests. And why? I ask. To talk shop, of course, than which there is no keener pleasure.

I should like to be able to say as much of my author colleagues—for I am in the unusual situation of having two professions which I love equally but practise unequally. Of course, I know authors who cannot conceal their enthusiasm and who discuss professional matters eagerly whenever they have a chance. But I want to make it clear that when I speak of "shop," I am not thinking of the gossip that is common to all such societies, of the minor grievances against publishers and editors of newspapers, and all the inevitable but comparatively unimportant dealings with agents; no, I am thinking of our art, our message, and our mission, and I am speaking of those invigorating difficulties we encounter in trying to express and to control our ideas and our material; I am thinking of that bitter conflict between inspiration and style which is our daily penance.

One of my superior friends will probably tell me that this conflict is too intimate to be a subject even of friendly discussion ... and that reserve and modesty ... and so on. Right! I like solitude as much as anyone, and I suspect idle conversation. But when men meet together, even intelligent men, they are almost certain to talk nonsense or to drop into political gossip or local scandal. Therefore all honor to the profession which provides an inexhaustible subject of sensible conversation, the profession which saves us from talking twaddle, the profession that gives us something that is really worth discussion.

I am not forgetting that in literary circles there are prigs and poetasters of every description who, under pretense of talking about their profession, always contrive to talk about themselves. We can avoid these gentlemen, and when we meet together we must not be afraid to discuss the subjects that are closest to our hearts. I do not personally like "interviews," but I shall welcome them if they really force writers to speak and think about their profession and to ponder the intricacies and mysteries of their art.

One of the calamities of this confused epoch is the indifference of people in every walk of life to the work they have to do. It is a natural result of the machine age, and I want to be careful not to offer the slightest suggestion of reproach to those people who will henceforward have to go on working without the reward of enjoying what they do. The Russian novelists assure us that the workmen of the new regime sincerely love their trades and are encouraged to do so; for the honor of mankind I hope that this may be so, and that this idea is not simply another theoretical conclusion from the makers of five-year plans.

We who are members of the liberal professions, who have the joy and the honor and the privilege of accomplishing work we like, freely chosen by ourselves, we ought, in spite of present difficulties, at least to take the trouble to honor the profession which has made us what we are.

VII

TRADE UNIONISM. LIMITS OF SYNDICALISM

I AM at home in my study.

The person who is holding forth on the other side of the table is a well-known writer. He has an appointment with me, and we have been talking for five minutes while I am waiting for him to come to business.

After a smile and a short silence he comes to the point.

"I have come to you because I and some friends intend to found an authors' syndicate, and we wanted first to get your agreement in principle."

"But," I replied, thanking him with a gesture, "there are several professional associations of which one, at least, the Société des Gens de Lettres, is excellent. It does its work well and with discretion; by this I mean that it does not exceed its powers, or better still, keeps within its duties."

"Exactly. . . ."

"Are you suggesting that it should exceed them?"

"No, of course no. But we are of the opinion that as well as such a society, with its rather limited powers, there is room for a closer group with a more ambitious program, a group actuated by the true syndicalist ideal."

"Yes, perhaps. And what do you mean by the syndicalist ideal?"

My visitor put on a serious expression and raised a finger heavenwards, as if to declare his creed.

"By the syndicalist ideal I mean an ideal devoted entirely to our corporate interests."

"You realize that such interests are many-sided, and that spiritual and temporal desires do not always march side by side."

"All the more reason for giving equal attention to both. On the temporal side our syndicate will offer its members mutual assistance in practical ways that are yet to be discussed; on the spiritual side it will keep an eye on literary usage, stand for all that is highest and best in the art, interest itself in certain disputes and not be afraid to take sides when our common honor is at stake; and so on. . . ."

"Yes."

"Well, may we count on your support in principle?"

The speaker's face expressed quiet confidence.

"Just a minute," I said, "we will discuss this business again in a few days' time. You must let me turn it over in my mind."

I have done so.

The world is large, quite large enough, whatever the descendants of Malthus may say, to feed and to house all men of goodwill and possibly a few doubtful specimens as well. For literature to be representative it means that authors of very different gifts and talents and ambitions and styles must work each at his own level on the slopes of the sacred mountain. I repeat, men of apparently contrary virtues, men who cannot understand each other and yet must collaborate with more or less success, more or less happiness, more or less perseverance, to the glory of their art and the further-ance of their ideals. In my opinion it is a good thing that men of different types, each with his place in the sun, should be trying not only to keep that place but to extend and improve it.

I am naturally tolerant and I hate eclecticism. A few books I love, a number I admire, and a still greater number I like. But we all have our foibles, and our power for love is mixed with a power for hate. There are some works that I detest, and there are some authors whose output seems to me to be tiresome or even poisonous.

"Corporate interests," my visitor said. I suppose I have some interest or other in common with every man on this earth, and I certainly have many in common with the writers whose work I admire. But there are some writers whose interests, if I may put it so, awake no interest in me. We have the obstinate idea, some of us, that the interests of art somehow rise a flight above our "trade union" interests, we even believe that the supreme interest of our "union" is to be found in the glory of art; rightly or wrongly we are persuaded that the cause of art, our art, is one with the cause of the spirit—co-extensive with the cause of mankind. Yet for the assessment of those who purport to serve this cause we can count on no supernatural sign but simply on the light of our own reason, which is willful and fallible, and ultimately on our personal taste, which is fierce, mad, even quite unjust, yet indomitable.

Laborers, artisans, tradesmen, and manufacturers, all the people who are engaged in trade, are organized in powerful unions. The professional classes, the schoolmasters and the doctors, have followed suit. I am told, and indeed it is obvious, that the trade union spirit has overcome all sorts of obstacles, has imposed the authority of corporations, and has safeguarded the interests of individuals during disputes. All this is admirable in my opinion, admirable in the main, but with a few reservations.

The reason why the artistic world has not joined in this remarkable, almost triumphal movement is probably that its members have not, and never could have, a simple straightforward conception of this thing called the common interest; they cannot accept regulations blindly, and by the nature of their work they develop a frame of mind which is not susceptible to group discipline.

I find that I can do my duty to my neighbor (a free variety of trade union duty) with alacrity provided always that it does not seem, after close solitary scrutiny, to run counter to my artistic duty; which amounts to saying that a professional writer is not and can never be, from the trade union point of view, pure in heart in the sense of being free from preoccupations that are foreign to the trade union.

Fortunately such preoccupations are usually the expression of individual rebellion, and I believe they may even have value outside the restricted world of art and letters. It is conceivable that in certain organizations the best interests of a trade or business may not be sufficiently obvious to effect a modification in union

decisions—I am afraid that this is true. But if I were a
locksmith, and really in love with my work—this is not
a frivolous supposition, for I have been passionately
engaged in several professions at different times—I can
imagine that I might visualize the best interests of lock-
smithing so clearly as to have little sense of solidarity
with a locksmith *saboteur*—a bad locksmith.

I know that such ideas must haunt many honest
workmen and must sometimes trouble their union loy-
alties, but that everyday necessities usually nip them in
the bud. I know that individual desires and requirements have had to be sacrificed for the common good.
I know, too, that the closer one is to manual work the
harder it is to see a trade as a whole. Is the builder more
important than the building? Well, I should not like
to say; the question brings up the general consideration
of the sanctity of labor, that ancient and respectable
divinity; I could only say that a bad builder damages
the well-being of his craft as a whole.

Although we are far from the days of the "Children
of Solomon," the days of journeymen and apprentices,
trade unionism still makes a point of "professional
honor," and sets out to maintain a high level of *esprit
de corps,* if necessary by means of internal tribunals
and sanctions. In some cases, as, for example, in the
medical profession, the unions assume the right of cen-
soring and even punishing members who are found
guilty of offenses against deontology or professional
honor. It is evident that the function of the union
becomes more and more dangerous the nearer it gets to
matters of the spirit, and that is why unionism, when

it attempts to deal with the profession of letters, finds itself faced with insurmountable obstacles.

Let us imagine a literary trade union which has the courage to go beyond the domain of practical affairs, to weigh up men and their works, to determine questions of common sense, taste, morality, and art on behalf of the language as a whole. Into whose hands would such an organization fall, sooner or later? How would its formidable powers be exercised? One does not like to think; one sees a picture of Baudelaire expelled from the bosom of the union, Rimbaud refused admittance, Verlaine reprimanded, and Mallarmé subjected to repeated calls to order.

No, no; unionism, which has turned this century upside down, must pause at the threshold of literature. If it aims too low we will have nothing to do with it; if too high, we reject it at once. Heaven grant that it may forget us and leave us to our fate! Anything it could offer us is nothing compared with the demands it would make. We are the only individuals left in the world; let us hold out to the last in our trenches.

VIII

SIGNATURES AND MANIFESTOES

SOCIAL ideas over a period of time might be represented by an undulating graph. Some ideas are born, live for a while, then die forever; others revive obstinately, so that their existence is made up of alternating periods of favor and discredit.

The idea of fellowship which dominated the Middle Ages lost ground for a long time and then re-established itself. It has governed the end of the nineteenth century and the beginning of the twentieth, and no doubt it will fail in the future only through the very excess of its own victory.

I am no adversary of all forms of co-operative effort among the higher professions which are still called liberal—I say "still" because I am thinking of the ambitions and encroachments of nationalism. I am of the opinion, as I have just explained, that the spirit of fellowship in science, literature, and art should preserve individual freedom, and should confine its activity to practical problems, professional obligations, and the defense of a few important general principles about which there can be no dispute; that done, the individual should be allowed to keep his own pace and rhythm, his personal opinions, his sovereignty, in fact.

The power of the spirit is great, even in a society dedicated to the worship of mammon. The "temporals" know well enough that in order to keep their empire they must obtain the agreement of the "spirituals," or failing this must control them, or failing this again must lock them up or destroy them. There is no need in considering the power of the "spirituals"—note that I do not say of the spirit—to give way to exaggeration, neither is there cause for despair; this power is a real thing and is still taken account of by those who make a bid for leadership.

It is just because this power is real and closely concerns the leaders that they have tried to tie it down by the rules of arithmetic. Some people have thought, still think, and will long continue to think, that the spiritual power of ten good men is equal to ten times the power of each one of them. This, put in a new way, is the Bergsonian problem of the intensive and the extensive.

When the world is being shaken by great events the men who are able to pass judgment on these events, either because they have been witnesses of them, or because they have clarity of vision, or because they are strongly moved by horror and indignation, or because they possess high moral authority and the capacity to make themselves heard, have the right, and perhaps the duty, to bear evidence. Writers, for example, who took part in the War were well equipped to make a deposition, to write their memoirs, to describe people and things, to criticize the event, and thus arouse the public conscience.

So it is that the great events of history often cause

the "spirituals" to intervene and take action. When a well-informed man boldly throws the weight of his authority into a discussion, raises his voice on behalf of justice or mercy, and thus offers himself of his own free will as the advocate of a difficult and dangerous cause he commands our attention and respect and all the help we can give him. The signature of one of these men that I am calling "spirituals" is not only, as the word suggests, the "sign" of a mind and a character, of a talent or a genius, but represents in addition a whole life, a whole lifework, of which the working capital is the confidence and respect that have gradually been accumulated through the years.

Such a signature, even when it is rash and intemperate, always touches me, urges me to thought, enlists my sympathy, and arms me for battle.

But I assert, with the weight of long experience, that these signatures are not susceptible to simple arithmetical addition.

For the last twenty-five years manifestoes with collective signatures have been abused in all countries. I have signed a great number myself. I am really well informed about this phenomenon and therefore I can speak freely. Many of these manifestoes, organized to protest against miscarriages of justice, are very worthy, in my opinion; I make no criticism of their matter or their manner; but their efficacy seems to me to be doubtful.

The people I have just been calling "spirituals," as opposed to "temporals," are luckily, whether they will or no, distinct individualists. Their opinions are never exactly the same as anyone else's, even their brother's or their wife's or their best friend's. They know what they think and they say it outright. Moreover they have a pen which is at the service of their sentiments and their faith, and their signature, as they well know, stands for a mind which if not solitary is at least unique.

Then we ask them for their signature—that signature which is ordinarily jealously reserved for works that have been laboriously conceived and pondered word by word. We ask them to put their signature to a text that has been conceived and worded by a stranger. We ask them and they do it. Why?

In the first place because the proposals put forward appeal, at any rate in some respects, to the feelings of the person approached. Usually agreement is not whole-hearted. The signatory would like, if he could, and if he had the time and the inclination—I do not say the right because that would further complicate the argument—to correct certain paragraphs, to change words, to rearrange the presentation of ideas and arguments. But he has not time, nor perhaps inclination, and practically never the opportunity. He shrugs his shoulders and signs, with or without hesitation. Very often the manifesto moves him, bowls him over perhaps, fires his blood. Certainly he would prefer a different wording, but it cannot be helped—better get it signed and sealed and off in the post.

The signature is not always given with enthusiasm, and it may be subsequently renounced. The manifesto may have been presented through a friend, or perhaps by an enemy to whom one wants to appear to be a good sport; persuasion and surprise operate in many cases and other factors intervene such as the fear of not doing as others do, anxiety not to displease an influential body, and sometimes that form of cowardice which arises from the fear of appearing cowardly.

I believe that many who sign a manifesto do so through weakness, indifference, ignorance, good nature, curiosity, to be left in peace, to be in the swim, in fact, for a thousand reasons that have nothing to do with reason.

Let us be clear on this point. It is important that the "spirituals" shall not renounce their power or their privileges. They have their pen and their public and they exercise authority. Let them use their power when they deem it to be opportune, but each one *alone,* because they are solitaries by vocation and by the necessities of their work. Let them write what they think and sign it proudly. But let them beware of collective signatures. Many of them will realize too late that they have made undertakings which are contrary to their deepest ideals; many will find that they will have to reverse their decisions, like some of those our Swiss friends used to call the "Ninety-three Intellectuals"; many will discover that their action has made them the innocent prey of political parties; many will be forced to admit that in renouncing their right to an individual opinion they are compromising just those very ideas that they most wish to serve, ideas which have nothing to do with chance associations and mass demonstrations.

It may be argued that manifestoes sometimes give an opportunity for opinions to be canvassed publicly. That is an over-simplification, because minds cannot be counted up like bricks or apples. I might add that these arbitrary reckonings only increase disorder and intensify disagreement.

We must beware of rash commitments. I do not say that I will never again put my signature to a manifesto, but I am firmly resolved to express my own opinion when it seems to be necessary as I have done a hundred times in the past. And at a time when mankind is giving way to collective excitements of all sorts it seems appropriate to remark that only man as an individual is worthy of my act of faith.

IX

THE SOCIAL FUNCTION OF THE WRITER

THE social function, as distinct from the many others that a man fulfills, is the one through which he responds to a need of society.

For most people in a normal society the demands of their work and their private lives are such that they have neither time nor energy to know the world in the philosophic and poetic sense, and to put the results of their discoveries into words. They gladly leave such matters to the specialist, that is to say, to the writer, who is thus given a mandate by society to make acts of cognizance to the best of his ability.

In my view a writer is fulfilling his social function when he helps us to a better understanding of the world and the people in it, when he devotes himself according to Paul Claudel's formula to "transforming the unknown into the known," when he is a discoverer and inventor, a detector who exercises his property of detection directly on human beings, events, phenomena, or indirectly on the thoughts and works of civilized man.

Such a function, which has always been indispensable to the proper development of a harmonious society, can only bear fruit in an atmosphere of justice and liberty. Now liberty has definite limits. Strongly individualistic though I am I do not forget that I live in society; therefore in estimating the liberty that is conceded to me I am willing to make certain personal sacrifices. I should say that there is a reasonable supply of liberty when I see that the great poets and philosophers, who are our acknowledged masters, can produce their work without constraint. If conditions were such that Goethe, Hugo, Dante, Montaigne, Shakespeare, Cervantes, and Spinoza would be in chains, then I should say that I am not free. That is my criterion.

Restrictions against liberty have not always prevented writers from doing creative work but they have spoiled the relations between writers and society. In other words, they have distracted the writers in the exercise of their lawful social function.

Any word that has been in use for a long time acquires new meanings more or less distinct from the original meaning which must be examined and defined if one wants to pursue a line of thought or institute a discussion.

The social function of the writer in the sense that I have just defined it does not admit of much controversy; but it is quite another matter if I give the word "social" its modern connotation.

The expression "social function" had originally, to my ear, the simple meaning I have just given it. I must add that for most people today the word "social" has a political sense. Thus the social function of the writer may signify the part that he will eventually play on the political stage.

Rigorous adherence to definition would bring this discussion to nothing, because in social politics a writer as such has not, and could not have, anything that could strictly be called a function. In a well-constructed society sociology and politics would be left to competent experts who would be carefully chosen and experienced men. A writer may see his duty in this special domain; may take his orders so to speak; but his real function, I repeat, is something quite different.

Having thus defined the terms of our discussion I add that it is useless to dismiss a problem which is daily being forced on our attention. It is not a new problem, and the trend of events makes it more urgent than ever today. Therefore we must tackle it squarely. I think it may be stated as follows: Should a writer become personally involved in politics, and more especially in class warfare?

History has supplied many answers. Many great writers, famous in their profession, have not been afraid to take part in politics, nor have they been afraid to put their personal ability and their literary reputation at the disposal of their parties. Some have taken part for love of the game, others out of a taste for battle and power, others, again, out of a disinterested sense of justice. These and other motives may operate in individual cases, for every writer is the sole judge of his own behavior. Our task now is to formulate a general principle from the facts.

Those who advocate action can quote illustrious examples from history. The writer, they say, in his position as spectator and critic, is unworthy of his profession unless he puts his ability and his influence and his personality at the service of the righteous cause, of the oppressed against their oppressors, indeed, of humanity as a whole.

Few writers remain unmoved by this simple argument, and most poets, because their peculiar gifts have taught them to search for truth underneath outward appearance and to express it in stirring words, are deeply conscious of their responsibility. When they have been actors in or spectators of an event they try to reproduce it, not merely as a work of art, but as an act of testimony. When they have only indirect knowledge of certain facts they reserve the right to express an opinion and to deliver a public verdict. This liberal attitude, which is not without risks, wins general acceptance and the pedant who refuses to take sides appears not as an apostle of freedom but rather as a prisoner of his own egotism.

That is roughly how the question appeared to our grandfathers in the age of romanticism; since then it has become much more complicated.

The political parties, especially since the beginning of this century, have made great efforts to persuade scholars and artists and writers to take action. Politicians are fully aware of the popular reputation enjoyed by some authors, and they do all they can to get hold of such valuable cards in the game; writers are solicited daily, especially by the parties of the extreme left and right.

As I have already pointed out they often have pertinent reasons for acceding to these requests. Some plunge in with enthusiasm, others out of friendship, others yield weakly. Professional pride may be a deciding factor—authors are told that they are relied on to say something, and so they stand up and let themselves be heard.

Encouraged by good results the politicians, who for the most part have no respect for the artistic world, exploit the generosity of the writers cynically. Every day authors are asked to express opinions on subjects of which they know practically nothing, and on people whom they know only at second hand. These requests are sometimes peremptory—they may become a menace.

This state of affairs is most damaging to the cause of literature and authors are in danger of losing the authority they have so painfully acquired, with no one any the better for it. Our profession may fall into disrepute through having presumed too much on its power and prestige; which would be a great misfortune.

Does this mean that in these difficult circumstances a conscientious writer should abstain? Such is certainly not my idea.

Like aloes which wait for years before flowering, writers should patiently investigate the cases they intend to assess. They should long collect their thoughts before speaking, speak at the right moment, and say no more than is actually necessary. Only so will they have a chance of using their power effectively and successfully. They must turn a deaf ear to the solicitations of factions and politicians, refuse to do commissioned work, and eschew log-rolling.

"Alone and free to accomplish his mission," said

Vigny. I see no reason for modifying that maxim today. The poet added: "Only solitude is holy." How well this fine phrase illuminates the position of those of us who, not content to drift aimlessly, take our bearings daily on the map of the universe!

X

POLITICAL WRITINGS

We were still very young when we first heard the cry "Politique d'abord!" which might have been a word of command, a statement of fact, or a prophecy. We heard it with dismay.

It was the beginning of the twentieth century. France, still ringing with the Dreyfus *affaire,* was by no means unpolitical, and the law separating Church and State had just roused angry passions throughout the country. We were emerging from our colonial adventures, uneasy but flushed with success. The weekly bombs of the Russian nihilists echoed down the corridors of Europe, but particularly of France. The spirit of trade unionism was fostering strikes and demonstrations. The Frenchman of that time was by no means uninterested in public affairs; but he did not subordinate all his thought and action to them—he still knew how to look after himself.

At that time students in the laboratories were eagerly discussing the ideas of Le Dantec, Dastre, and Richet, and to students of philosophy the name of Bergson was a master-word, which would dispel all lesser ideas. We who were beginning our career as writers devoted ourselves heart and soul to the cult of the masters we had chosen. One cannot think without regret of the splendid youthful fervor which could discuss philosophy or poetry or morality while instinctively avoiding the rhetorical style and the odious vocabulary of public meetings. It was a time when the Académie française could give its highest literary prize with a good grace to the author of *Jean Christophe* and when he could accept it with genuine pleasure. Yet the *Affaire* was only just over and we were on the eve of the World War. But we still knew how to detach our minds from politics for work and play, how to seek sanctuary in that mystic ark of which Descartes has given us so ingenious a model.

Things have changed very much since then. The phrase "Politique d'abord," originally a mere slogan, has now become a painful reality and politics occupy the forefront of every mind. I fully realize that political anxiety is daily becoming more urgent and more tragic. But it will soon supplant all other activities, and when I think of the possibilities of the human mind I say that this is a great misfortune.

Every day in addition to letters, newspapers, reviews, and papers of all sorts I get a certain number of books. The same applies to all my author colleagues. It may be that the professional critics, more favored than I, reap a still richer harvest. I must say that my share is nothing to complain of. I get stories, novels, biographies realistic and romantic, legends, poetry, works of scholarship, science, and philosophy. From all this mass I choose what I need for my mental diet. I keep no statistics—I have neither the ability nor the inclination—but

I observe in general terms the frequency or rarity of certain types of work and the good and bad examples of each species.

What strikes me most is the abundance of works of a political nature. Of course, politics is a vast subject stretching from economics to morality, and has many faces and many masks from that of the most austere philosophy to libel and scandal; but even taking this into consideration there is no doubt that works of a political character absorb an excessive, and in that sense abnormal, proportion of the mass of printed matter.

One day last winter I received three or four brochures each drawing my attention to a plan for reforming the national regime and the social system—in fact, for world reform. The little works I am referring to now have nothing to do with the memoranda and pamphlets published and broadcast in such numbers by the political agents—they are either the work of isolated individuals or else they are printed under the aegis of little groups of people, newly formed and with practically no contacts with the parliamentary groups. It is easy to see that some of these people, in order to bring their scheme to the light of day, have made real personal sacrifices, spent their savings heroically, played all their trumps. In some cases, a lively regard for the public well-being is apparent, a sincere desire for the re-establishment of order and safety. Criticism and satire are notable by their absence, and the effort is usually directed towards stability and construction rather than towards denigration and destruction.

Naturally these discourses tend to be naïve. Next door to some ingenious argument one encounters puerile formulae strongly resembling the well-known and well-tried ones. For example, the writer proposes to "rebuild in an atmosphere of confidence," or "to establish order founded on justice," or "to reform the fiscal system on a basis of simplification and equity." Who in France would seriously oppose such ideas?

But, criticism apart, I maintain that this extraordinary flood of political writings is a symptom of the utmost gravity.

I know that the French people are fond of politics, in practice and in theory. In France politics and love are the two pleasures of the poor, free to all. Drinks cost money, but politics cost nothing and are intoxicating—they have their thrills, they excite our instincts, they offer us expectancy and occasional satisfaction, and they thrive on all the passions, especially the lowest. A suitable entertainment for empty minds when the newspaper is exhausted. Yes, the French are great armchair politicians and always have been, even in their peaceful days.

But when the political fever takes the turn it has today and attacks people who by taste and occupation should be immune, when every citizen spends his spare moments or his sleepless nights building a new state, single-handed, with rage in his heart, then I say from the point of view of a doctor there is evidence of profound disorder in our social life.

I concede that politics should be a profession with us, as in other countries, and that in our modern highly specialized society politics should be left to the professionals. But at least let them in performing their function relieve us of anxiety.

A state of health, in the physiological sense, is characterized by the fact that the possessor no longer thinks about his body. The healthy man takes certain daily precautions and looks after his constitution; he eats and drinks and washes and goes off to his business. Does he cross-examine himself anxiously every hour or every minute about the state of his pancreas or his suprarenal glands? Not a bit of it. He may not even know the names or situations of these organs. The moment he begins to think about his stomach it means that his stomach is out of order. If the trouble persists he is well advised to consult a specialist—that is to say, a doctor. He is wise, too, to trust his specialist and to accept his injunctions. But when the patient begins to look up medical books and popular encyclopedias and anxiously, indignantly perhaps, to prescribe for himself and to visualize imaginary operations, then I say that things are going badly with him, and that the outlook is black.

In a well-ordered society an ordinary man need give no more time to politics than to his daily toilet—less if anything. When I went to Russia in 1927 I was immediately struck by what I might call their political intemperance. The Russian who wanted to do his duty—I say "wanted" because things may be changed now; they move very fast in Russia—had to devote several hours a day to what Jacques Rivière used to call "the Soviet phenomenon," that is to say, an act of corporate thinking. I am sure that public well-being is in no need of such strenuous assistance.

With specialist workmen and officials in their proper places the citizen of a well-governed country ought to be able to forget politics almost entirely. If he does not forget them but thinks about them continuously and gloomily, then the disease is serious and the remedy ineffective.

France has resisted this deadly infection for a long time, but at last she has fallen a victim. The few independent spirits who have not given up hope of interesting their contemporaries in the problems of science and art and literature and philosophy are not slow to realize that these fundamental considerations no longer interest anyone. Politics are like garlic, so strong a flavoring that the very best food tastes insipid without it.

A nation which has to devote the best part of its time and energy to political matters, whether by force or of its own free will, seems to me to be a decadent nation. Even supposing that it maintains its credit and its temporal power it can no longer produce those great geniuses who must live exempt from mob servitudes, prejudices, and work-to-order, if they are to bear fruit. And a nation is only great when it produces great men.

XI

TEMPORAL POWER

I AM speaking only of literature, but the theories I am about to put forward apply equally well to any career involving creative effort.

By temporal power I mean all power that is exterior to man, all power that is added to a man's natural worth and is of such a nature as to affect his authority, his influence, and his behavior. Such power may be justified by certain spiritual attainments or it may hide a notable lack of them. I should say that a writer is exercising a sort of temporal power when he is managing a newspaper or a review, when he is directing or advising a publishing house or editing a series of books, when he has a post in certain types of business or serves on special committees, when he belongs to academic and professional bodies, and finally when he has the formidable advantage of capital inherited or acquired.

I am leaving on one side for the moment this question of personal fortune because it requires a special investigation. Besides, it is a problem that may disappear tomorrow, at any rate temporarily, in the welter of social and political upheavals. But the problem of external influence, of the uses and functions of temporal power, can be examined at leisure, for it is a problem for all eternity.

If one of my sons were to show a tendency towards a literary career—a thing I do not desire, nor do I see any signs of it at present—I should give him the benefit of my knowledge and experience.

I should tell him that the life of an author or an artist, that is to say, of a man who attempts to create works of value, is first and foremost an experiment, or, if you prefer it, a test. The great thing for you, I should say, is firstly to give your gifts free play, to develop them and refine them and discover your bent, and then to get to understand them so as to be able to apply them most effectively. Every work is an end and a means; yes, I mean what I say; a means of accomplishing some day a work that shall be higher and more difficult and consequently better. If you accept these simple principles, you ought to try to live in such a way as to acquire your experience of life in as rigorous a manner as possible. It is not a question of morals—your personal interest is at stake. You want to know what you are worth, recognize your failings, weigh up the rewards of your labor correctly, so beware of anything which may invalidate your calculations or warp your judgment.

You are not rich and you will soon have to earn your living. Therefore learn a trade and try to make a decent living at it without expending all your energies, since in your secret heart you are dedicated to literature. This need for a second profession will be accepted by all right-thinking men in future. Do what you want, and what you can, but go on with your foster-profession as long as may be necessary so that you need ask nothing from literature until luck decides in your favor. Avoid especially those para-literary and quasi-literary activities which will spoil your style, exhaust your inventive faculties, and force you into jobs for which you are not fitted. When you have an idea for a work and the time and the inclination to do it, give to it all your energy—but do not forget to live. There is always time, plenty of time, for writing when you are in the twenties; live intensely for three months in order to write for three days and produce three pages.

Your early efforts may be noticed—it is possible even that luck will brush you with its wings. Perhaps everything is going perfectly—now is the time to think about temporal power, for temptation will soon be upon you.

I can hear the common-sense man saying: "I am well off the mark; I am being talked of as a success, offered recognition, a status, possibly a post. This will all be a help to me in my artistic career and will give me the prestige I need."

Well, I am not so sure. The first necessity of a good writer is to be read, and I should add to be read in aseptic conditions. This is by no means an easy matter. The author once he is launched on this extraordinary career wants to be read by a public of whom he has a preconceived idea, the audience of his choice, that ideal audience for whom he writes every word and every thought. It needs patience to convert an audience, and one of the hardest parts of his task is to be read by his fellow-authors—this is the most difficult thing in the world and yet an essential condition of ultimate success. It is necessary for your colleagues to read your works and judge them. If you really want to know what your gifts are worth and what is the significance of your work, do not ask for and do not accept any share of temporal power until the hard years of apprenticeship are over.

How can you hope to be criticized impartially if you command influence other than that of your own personality? Be deaf to entreaty and beware of spite. Show yourself naked before your judges, naked, at peace, and with nothing except your works in your hands.

Resist temptation and persevere; listen, observe, and take your bearings every day. Try to discover the direction of your work and your life. If your conscience remains clear you will know just how much praise and criticism is worth and you will fortify yourself against them both; and you will work throughout the greater part of your life with a feeling of security.

Perhaps one day you will begin to think that you know something about yourself. A day will certainly come when you will have gathered a rich experience from your work; a day will come, I hope, when you will be about fifty years old. You have worked hard and will have a big output behind you. You will enjoy a position that you owe solely to the work of your mind. If when this moment comes you think you can usefully employ your knowledge in the cause and service of literature, then offer it ten, twenty, a hundred times, and if you believe you have the necessary strength of mind accept some share of temporal power. But realize that it must always be a bitter experience and so be careful, be prudent.

XII

THE FACULTY OF INVENTION

TIRED of gazing at the white paper, so the story goes, Jules Renard used to wander the streets hoping for inspiration from the thousand sights around him. Sometimes this chaser of rainbows, afraid of returning empty-handed, used to call on Rachilde in the hope of striking a spark from him, and would go away satisfied.

The faculty of invention, of creating stories and re-arranging the elements of life in a new pattern, the power of making fictitious characters live and speak with a personality of their own, is undoubtedly the most stubborn of all the virtues. One can train oneself to patience, to courage, to strength, even to subtlety, but one can neither call up nor compel the power of invention.

Anyone who is endowed in whatever degree with this precious gift ought to make use of it, putting it to the test of action and fulfilling it in his work; he must also guard against its corruption and annihilation.

The young writers in France today are well educated and splendidly keen, and they go in for journalism of all sorts with energy and sincerity. I approve of their being asked to write articles and essays and criticisms and reports and stories and so on. But I say categorically that the hundred-line short story published daily by almost all the French newspapers is a mistake, and that it is doing serious damage to the inventive faculty of a nation who have always been considered to be good story-tellers.

The ideas and the mental images that make suitable material for a work of art always ripen slowly. They are born in us like larvae and for a long time they show no sign of life; little by little we feel them growing and taking shape within us. Then they begin to move and torment us; years pass; at last the fictitious being is ready for the light of day and a painful delivery begins. At this stage everything may yet be ruined, but if we have allowed a proper period of incubation we have at least a chance of bringing into the world a creation that will be alive, a living entity, properly formed.

Everyone who has some experience of writing knows that he may have waited ten years, perhaps more, before trying to depict such and such a character, before bringing such and such a picture to light, before liberating such and such an idea or story.

I believe that the short story which is in such favor today in nearly all the daily papers is a sterile art and likely to be fatal to the creative spirit; sterile because it does not stimulate or impregnate the writer's talents while he is actually writing; and fatal because it is likely to destroy the author who lends himself to it.

I have reflected at length before broaching this subject which is so important for the life of the mind and the future of literature. The art of the short story is a difficult one. The reader who turns through a collection of Maupassant will be surprised to discover that next to an excellent story, rich and well developed and giving its title to the volume, may be concealed mediocre tales, redolent of journalism. Maupassant has sinned against the fundamental laws of that art of which he is a master. Pressed for time he has cut his hay green. For his hundreds of published stories he had matter enough for only thirty (a number which would be enough for most men). This famous example is not one to be followed. At the rate things are going the demands of journalism are likely to exhaust the inventive faculty of a vigorous generation without doing any good to anyone.

"An idea glows in the recesses of the soul, a strong living idea which in years to come may develop into the material for a whole work; this idea is our secret treasure and we do not want to sacrifice it at the altar of Moloch. But time passes and batters us. We have to supply two stories a month to a newspaper. The date approaches, it is on us. A few hours still remain, but we have nothing to say, nothing to tell. There are dark days when the brain is dry and hard—not the tiniest little anecdote, not the suggestion of a plot, not the least shadow on the broad screen of memory. Are we going to draw on our last reserve, that favorite story so long cherished? Nothing else to be done with time knocking at the door—we go and dash off a hundred lines on this theme that is so dear to us, this theme that might have become our masterpiece."

In my opinion the daily story is one of the black spots in our literary life, an open wound which is losing good blood.

Some people may raise the objection that writers who thus prostitute their talent do not deserve to be saved. That is wrong thinking. I know and I can name distinguished writers who have been ruined by this short story telling. Occasionally, too, I happen to read one of these papers thrown to the winds by a young unknown writer, and I feel as if I am witnessing a suicide—though I admit this is rare because out of a thousand stories squandered on the daily press not more than three are worth re-reading.

Like everyone else nowadays I have published some stories in the papers; I understand the evil I am describing and trying to overcome. I know that many writers have to make a living for themselves and their families and that it breaks their heart to make it in such a manner. I well understand that the question is not a simple one. I intervene because of my deep concern for literature and writers. I believe that writings about ideas and facts and men and their works may be multiplied with impunity and the writer who follows up a question that interests him runs no risk of exhaustion—on the contrary he renews his energy. But a man who is forced to turn out half-fledged stories at all costs is, in my estimation, a victim and a martyr.

The public taste is becoming jaded by excess and we are breeding inattentive readers, satisfied with thin stories that have no psychological necessity and no strength of form. I regard this state of affairs as damaging both to popular taste and to the creative energy of our small army of writers.

XIII

ON ORIGINALITY

WE were lunching at our hotel one rainy day in São Paulo, that "city of tentacles" which fair Brazil has dedicated to the voracious gods of modern civilization. My companion was an author who was evidently inspired by the spirit of his great city and spoke enthusiastically of its future. "We are trying to build a new culture," he said, "strong and original and purely Brazilian...." My friend embarked on his theme with burning eloquence, and I listened with close attention and not without astonishment.

I often observed this ferment, this desire for an "original culture," during my travels in South America. The meetings organized at Buenos Aires by the International Institute for Intellectual Co-operation have discussed this problem at length. All who joined in this discussion recognized that the civilization imported into South America by its European conquerors has undergone notable modifications, but that, taken as a whole, the cultural values which form the basis of this new world remain very close to those of old Europe.

A few intellectuals in Latin America wisely accept this relationship, which can hardly be called a subordination. It does not matter much, they say, whether the new world borrows its ideas and its values from the old or not; the important thing is that the new world should be thinking and working. That it is doing so is undeniable.

Others, with a harshness which, in my opinion, is inopportune, criticize the superficiality of the new culture. Such people deliberately look to Europe as their intellectual home, and pin all their faith in Europe in spite of her mistakes and shortcomings.

Others again, disheartened by the way Europe is behaving, long to shake themselves free of their unreasonable mistress. They think that the time has come for the genius of the new peoples to launch proudly on a new career, and to create what they call an original culture. That was what my friend at São Paulo thought. In reporting his view I must add that this important problem is taken very coolly in Brazil. Most of the intellectuals I have met there seem to expect much the same from Europe as they have had since the time of the conquest. But Brazil is not the whole of South America, and writers like M. Teran have publicly expressed their hope of seeing Spanish America liberated from Europe and European traditions and set free to march forward to new and unknown destinations. In the years to come this view may well take on a mystical color, in which case it will radically change the relations between Europe and the young republics of the south.

While it is true that such a separation might be effected deliberately how can the pepole so "liberated" hope to develop the "original culture" which they long for?

It is immediately apparent that an original culture

is not, and never can be, the result of a deliberate decision.

Like faith it cannot be summoned at will, for culture is the product of a number of contributory circumstances for which science has not yet discovered the exact recipe. However, we know what some of the ingredients of the recipe are and the South Americans have conscientiously assembled them. Argentina, Uruguay, and Brazil—I am mentioning only those countries of which I have personal knowledge, but I ought also to include the others—have built numerous schools, many of them very fine. These countries have excellent schoolmasters and wonderfully equipped institutions and universities. Their liberal politics give every man a chance to display his talents. The foundation of a great culture has been laid and the preparatory work has already begun to bear fruit. Better results will follow, but no one can say when. They have now to watch and pray, that is to say, to work with energy and faith.

For a culture to be described as original it means that original methods must give rise to original works. Given the essential material conditions what is the next step? I should reply unhesitatingly, imitation. I mean, of course, imitation of great minds and established masterpieces. For a new order of society imitation is the only school of originality. It is humiliating only for minds that are ill-formed or presumptuous. La Fontaine published his most famous works under the title *Fables choisies mises en vers par M. de La Fontaine.* And that means, as the preface willingly admits, *Fables d'Ésope, choisies,* etc. Who would suggest for a moment that La Fontaine's work is not original? What we call the *Caractères* of La Bruyère were published by their author under the title *Caractères de Théophraste*. Shakespeare found his plots in Plutarch and Cinthio. Does this mean that La Bruyère is a second-class mind, or that Shakespeare is a second-rate poet? The question has already been answered. People who want to set up a new culture have only to follow the example of the best works of the old and famous cultures. Is this not precisely what Latin America has done, and wisely so, through the ages?

XIV

THE SPIRIT OF CONFUSION

WHILE events are daily emphasizing the moral disorder in which we are now forced to live it is interesting to observe the symptoms as reflected in certain disorders and epidemic diseases of language.

It is generally recognized that language, by virtue of the fact that it expresses the requirements of the mind, necessarily reflects its sorrows, its lapses, and its failings. Some of these failings are permanent and common to mankind as a whole, others are temporary and relate to historical circumstances. Anyone who listens daily to the conversation of his fellowmen must ask himself various questions to which answers can be found with the help of logic and the largely intuitive faculty called common sense.

Grammarians have long deplored the gradual disappearance of the interrogative form. They explain this phenomenon by various learned arguments to which I do not pay particular attention, because if the interrogative form is really disappearing it is probably because of a change or deterioration in mental outlook. But let us first examine the facts of the case.

In French a correct interrogative sentence necessitates a particular construction which is completed at the end of the phrase by a question mark. Thanks to this construction the reader has no need to go on to the sign at the end of the sentence in order to be able to give the phrase its proper intonation.

It is clear that this characteristic and indispensable construction is cordially disliked by the majority of people in France. I believe myself that laziness has a lot to do with this attitude. In order to pronounce such a sentence as "Que dites-vous?" correctly it needs a sort of sporting courage which most of our countrymen reserve for the boxing ring, or the football ground, or the cycle track. It is much easier to say curtly, "Vous dites?" with a light suggestion of interrogation in the voice. But laziness is not the primary factor in this business—the evil is more serious and deeper hidden.

Most people who use the affirmative or negative construction instead of the interrogative in my opinion betray a desire to conceal their ignorance. For example, you offer a good Burgundy to someone who does not know much about wine yet is anxious not to behave like an outsider; he sips the precious liquor with all the usual grimaces and then with an air at once detached and knowing drops one of the following phrases:

"C'est du Bourgogne?"

"C'est du Bordeaux?"

"Ce n'est pas du Châteauneuf?"

The intonation is so managed in each case that the *amour-propre* of the speaker has a possible line of retreat. The dialogue may proceed on several different lines:

"C'est du Bourgogne?"

"Oui, c'est du Bourgogne."

"C'est bien ce que je pensais."

Or perhaps:

"C'est du Bordeaux?"

"Non, c'est du Bourgogne."

"Évidemment, je m'en doutais."

Or again:

"Ce n'est pas du Châteauneuf du pape?"

"Oh! non, c'est du Bourgogne."

"Bien sûr, c'est du Bourgogne."

The man who is not trying to pretend that he knows everything would ask simply:

"Quel est ce vin?"

and under certain circumstances he might add:

"Est-ce du Bourgogne?"

or

"N'est-ce pas là du Bourgogne?"

It must be clearly understood that by the use of the interrogative construction, direct or indirect, the speaker admits his ignorance and his need of information. The man of the twentieth century will rarely admit his ignorance. Thanks to the press, to popular science and literature, to instructional films and broadcast speeches, the man of today is cocksure about everything. Of what use to him is the interrogative construction, which, in his view, is pretentious and difficult to speak, a vestige of the ages of obscurantism when mankind, knowing nothing, was obliged to ask questions about everything? Without the slightest doubt the time is coming when people of the present generation, hearing someone ask a question in the strict interrogative form, will say lowering their voices in commiseration: "C'est une faute? Parfaitement, je m'en doutais."

This spirit of self-sufficiency and mental confusion is apparent in other usages, both in words and turns of phrase. Many good writers abuse certain expressions which may not be wrong in themselves but are slightly vague.

It is not wrong to write "Une espèce de ... Une sorte de ..." but one becomes tiresome if one writes it too often. The man in the street uses such phrases not only too frequently but positively wrongly. He says "Un espèce d'imbécile." The fault of language is venial and trifling, but much more serious in my opinion is the state of mind that constant use of such errors brings about. With a few exceptions an established language like French, with its illustrious record and its ample supply of words, has a precise word for each object. The speaker who says "C'est une espèce de ..." betrays carelessness and haste, or inability to find the *mot juste,* or perhaps fear of the strength of the word and an unconscious desire to diminish its value. That is not "une espèce de lâcheté," it is cowardice itself.

The man of today is accentuating this bad habit, and is in a fair way to losing his sense of vocabulary. Not satisfied with weakening words he is allowing them to fall into oblivion. Objects of every conceivable sort are becoming simply *machines, choses,* and *trucs.* Even people are being lumped together, men under the term *machin* and women as *machine,* which seems to me to be a sinister anticipation. The Frenchman of the twentieth century has apparently forgotten that an essential function of the intelligence is to define entities and then classify them separately.

A man's character can be judged and the secrets of

his character revealed less by what he says than by the way he says it.

I once heard some business men talking and I had reason to suspect that they were trying to swindle each other. The subject matter of their conversation revealed nothing, but the turns of phrase betrayed them.

Words can be arranged in many different orders:

"Les premiers cent mille francs que j'ai gagnés..."

"Les cent premiers mille francs que j'ai gagnés..."

"Les cent mille premiers francs que j'ai gagnés..."

Finance would become really fair play if its investigations were conducted by grammarians with a little knowledge of psychology, and, of course, of medicine also.

XV

WEAKNESSES OF FAME

BUTCHERS are all rheumatic because they eat too much meat—they have to finish up what their customers have not bought. And writers, who may often be the blowers of their own trumpets of fame, play a fine part in the feast of noise. It is interesting to compare the reputation of an old scholar, covered with honors and decked with ribbons, with that of a young novelist who has published two little books representing six months of work and has won one of the literary prizes. I am often pained to see how my contemporaries cheerfully ignore such men as Charles Richet, Charles Nicolle, Dastre, and René Leriche, and I am only half consoled by the fact that names such as Arvers and Hégésippe Moreau are fairly well known.

If I thought that this inequality could hurt such men I should like to try to re-establish a little order and justice by confiding some of my secrets. A writer's fame is a brilliant thing, but that does not mean that it is reliable or lasting. I have published some fifty books and every day, in France or elsewhere, I meet well-meaning people who say: "Monsieur, I have read all your books!" I reply immediately: "That means that you have read four or perhaps one or two, and I am very pleased to hear it." Our conversation begins from that point.

Memory is a most enviable gift and teachers are quite wrong to neglect it, especially on behalf of their pupils. When people begin to talk to me about my books I know very well that they are full of literary enthusiasm, but their memory is by no means irreproachable. I often hear a remark such as "I particularly enjoyed your fine novel, *Les Civilisés*." I take care never to interrupt such a remark. Some time ago I published a book called *Civilisation*. Right. *Les Civilisés* is the book that rightly gained Claude Farrère his reputation. Besides, anyone can make a mistake—it is only a matter of one syllable. More often I am complimented on *Les Croix de bois;* in error there is always a modicum of truth; *Les Croix de bois* popularized Roland Dorgelès—but during 1917 I published a war book called *Vie des Martyrs*. When I am congratulated on *Les Croix de bois* I interpret it as *Vie des Martyrs* and all goes merrily.

Sometimes people are still further off the mark. One evening I was dining with a foreign diplomat, whose name I will not disclose, when the mistress of the house suddenly said to me affably: "Monsieur, I have read all your books. The one I like best is *Le Bal du comte Dorgelès*." After a few moments' hesitation I managed to establish the relationship along the following sequence: *Vie des Martyrs, Les Croix de bois, Dorgelès, Le Bal du comte Dorgelès*. So far so good. Sometimes the mistake arises not through a mistake in words but through the underlying meaning. In January last year my neighbor at table during a semi-official banquet was a famous foreign politician. "Monsieur," he thought he

had better say to me, "I have read all your books...
naturally, I like them all..." (a gracious little nod from
me) "but the one I like best is *Le Notaire du Havre*.
Of course, that is because I spent several years at Havre
during the War.... You understand, of course...." Oh,
yes, I understood all right and I laughed outright; for
in the book entitled *Le Notaire du Havre* there is nothing about Havre at all.

We were talking about mistakes of this sort one evening last year—a few writers among ourselves in a private house during one of my travels—when someone
came to warn me that a great political personage wanted
me to be presented to him. I yielded to the invitation,
and the statesman, whose manners were beyond reproach, said, after a moment or two: "Monsieur, I have
read all your books..." (slight nod from me); "the one
I like best is the one called *Les Crois de feu*" (I interpreted this as *Vie des Martyrs*, via *Les Croix de bois*,
Les Croix de feu).

I report these incidents, as I hope will be evident,
without any suggestion of mockery. It is no easy matter
to be gracious, and error is to be found everywhere,
at every turn and corner. Sometimes error itself makes
a mistake and then truth appears. But that is the exception that proves the rule. We live on "almost, but not
quite."

During the War I was once present at a cross-exami-
nation of a contingent of recruits. Admittedly they were
not the fine flower of youth; they were rather the sweep-
ings, gathered in from here, there, and everywhere, not
without difficulty, and an officer had the idea of giving
them a sort of examination. He asked them all: "Who

was head of the Government in France when the war of 1870 broke out?" The unfortunate men stood gaping, and I began to think that there would be no answer to the question; at last, the oldest of these lads, blushing, said hurriedly: "It was Badinguet." History was saved, but for a moment we had trembled for it. Fame, whether glorious or inglorious, has very narrow limits.

It always amuses me to remark on the errors of error. A few years ago before making a speech I was introduced by one of our ministers. I must admit that my chairman did his job nobly, and when the meeting broke up I thanked him sincerely. "Monsieur le Ministre," I said to him, and I was thinking only of the facts, "there were very few mistakes in that charming and graceful speech of yours."

In my opinion that was a remarkable tribute. Afterwards it was borne in on me that it was not appreciated quite as I had intended. But one cannot please everyone.

XVI

SHADOW PLAY

I saw Georg Brandes twice, at an interval of twelve years. I have sharp and exasperating recollections of these two meetings, and I cannot think of them without an access of impatience, almost of rancor; but eventually I managed to smile—bah, the old man is dead! It is high time to pin his picture to the wall and look at it without anger and without sentimentality.

I place the first of my two encounters during the winter of 1912-13, or perhaps in the spring of 1913. I could hunt up the correspondence and fix the date exactly, but it would be valueless; the only thing that needs remembering for the proper atmosphere is that it was before the War. I was twenty-eight years old. André Antoine had just produced my second play at the Odéon. It is called *Dans l'ombre des statues,* and the chief character is the son of a genius who is completely dominated by his father's greatness. The theme of this work appealed to Brandes the biographer of Goethe—I dare say he had pondered over the fate of the child that Goethe had by Christiane.

Thereupon Brandes came to Paris, signified that he wished to see me, and asked me to lunch with his host, André Rouveyre, that incisive artist with whom I was, and still am, on most friendly terms. I was excited at the thought of this meeting because in my eyes Brandes was one of the most remarkable minds in Europe—not creative, it is true, but powerfully critical and prodigiously erudite. He had met Ibsen and Tolstoy. He walked delicately in the kingdom of the mind—one of those omnivorous Jewish intelligences with limitless ramifications.

On my way to the rue Soufflot I remembered the kindly Verhaeren's story, of how staggered he was when, after he had been unctuously received by the German intellectual, and had been frank enough to make some fairly friendly remark on the Jewish question, he was apostrophized by Brandes in these surprising terms: "Surely you have not failed to notice, Verhaeren, that you are the only person here who is not a Jew?"

Thus my youthful curiosity that day was mingled with emotion and with alarm.

Brandes was nearly seventy. I was expecting to see an old man and Rouveyre had confirmed me in this impression by telling me that Brandes tired easily and so preferred lunch to dinner.

I could not then claim to be a connoisseur of the gradations of old age, but when Brandes appeared he astonished me. He was not tall, but erect and alert in every fiber. His hair and beard were thick and hardly graying; his eyes moved incessantly. He bade me be seated and plied me with a thousand questions. I will refer to the subject of these questions in a moment, but there is one more detail I must mention—Paul Fort was present at this very intimate meal, Paul Fort, our host, Brandes, and myself.

Famous men can hardly help being talkative; for how
can they resist all the people who beg for their words?
They are misers if they shut their mouths. To tell the
truth the loquacity of Brandes bowled me over completely. It was not a solemn monologue such as certain
pundits deliver, nor did it consist of neat squibs like
the talk of good story-tellers, nor of the fantasies, the
swift thrust and parry of the professional wits. No; it
was simply a running spate of gossip and scandal and
mischief-making. "Have you seen Madame de S——? Is
she as good-looking as they say? Does she sleep with
Monsieur C——? You don't know? Really? Do you go
to Madame R——'s? They say that she likes nice young
men herself, but her husband pinches them from her.
It's incredible. Do you believe it?" I imagined at first
that after this strange interrogatory—for I had the uncomfortable feeling of doing very badly in an examination—the old man would suddenly disperse these futile
visions with a gesture and devote himself to his memories of the great gods and the great demons, elaborate
a philosophy of art, a picture of intellectual Russia, a
history of the nineteenth century. But no, not a bit
of it—those were only my childish dreams! The great
man brought out not precious stones, but rubbish. He
went on rummaging for scandal, his eye sparkling, his
voice urgent. "They say that young C—— takes drugs.
... Have you seen enough of G—— to get an idea of
what his tastes are? No? Strange!"

The conversation lasted for three hours and left me
worn out. A few days later, just as he was about to leave
France, Brandes wrote me an ambiguous letter. He had
felt my discomfort and tried cynically to blame Paul

Fort for the turn the conversation had taken—I hasten
to add that there was absolutely no justification for this.

Then came the War and I had no difficulty in forgetting a picture of Brandes that I still wanted to think
was unfair and unrepresentative. The quarrels between
Brandes and Clemenceau did not affect me either way
—Brandes owed nothing of his fame to France and it
would be unreasonable to reproach him for his gratitude to Germany. The War came and went. In 1925 I
found myself in Copenhagen and I heard that Georg
Brandes wanted to see me, and had arranged for one
of his friends to invite me. It was an evening affair. I
had almost forgotten our first meeting. Brandes must
have got as old as Goethe and Hugo, I thought. I came
to this second meeting riper in mind, but no less keen
and inquisitive. There had been world-shaking events
—a good subject of conversation for this old spectator
of history.

I shall never forget Brandes's entrance that evening.
Shrunken, pink-skinned, white-haired, his eyes moist
with the cold, he came in, still very good-looking, and
groping his way said: "Where has Duhamel got to?" I
advanced to greet him. He made me sit next to him on
a divan; I was moved, and I awaited some august
remark.

And suddenly his old voice grew vibrant with its
everlasting prattle. "Do you know Madame Z——? No?
A pity. A most remarkable woman. You would meet
the comte de M—— at her house. Haven't you ever seen
him? Is it really possible?" Actually I knew the clothes-
peg in question, but I replied obstinately, "No, I don't
know him." Already the old man was off again. "Don't

you visit the G——'s? She is really a wonderful woman. Why don't you go there? The best conversation to be had in Paris, with the exception perhaps of Madame de C——'s. But surely you know Madame de C——?"

I shook my head furiously. At this point in our conversation, if Brandes had asked me whether I knew my own mother I should have shaken my head and said no.

For two or three hours the old man kept up this amazing twaddle, out of which Proust, I imagine, would have reaped a rich harvest. Finally wiping his moist eyes he said in a faint voice: "So you don't know anyone?"

I was keyed up, ready to bite him. But I respect old men, even when they are magnificently futile. I shook my head and said: "No; I know no one. And nothing."

A few months later Brandes died. I sometimes think of him in the evening after a day of solitude. Chaser of shadows! Collector of mists!

XVII

CONCERNING NAMES

A FEW years ago one of my young colleagues had the idea of using the name Duhamel for a character in a novel. At first I was somewhat taken aback. My friend evidently knew of my existence because he was then writing, or had just published, a small critical book about myself and my work and we were in good mutual relations. So I was surprised—nothing more. On consideration my surprise vanished, and to prevent the slightest chance of its reappearing—the young writer might have made his Duhamel a very boring person, for example—I refrained from reading the book, except for the first few pages. By this method I was able to preserve the indifference and sense of humor that is desirable in any discussion about names.

My name is an old French name which has survived in its medieval form. It comes from the north of France; in other places they use Dubourg, Dumas, Desmasures, Desmaisons, and so on. Of any thousand Frenchmen one at least will answer to the name of Duhamel, and I think there are four or five of us in the Larousse encyclopedia, and probably more than a hundred in the Paris directory, though I have not been to look. I have numerous namesakes to my own knowledge, all nice people as far as I know and sometimes very friendly. One of them who regularly receives a good proportion of my mail by mistake has been sending it to me for years with praiseworthy patience. So much so that I hardly know how to express my gratitude, for he even sends me back my own letters—but I should like to thank him all the same!

This simple and eloquent name naturally attracts story-tellers and dramatists. There is a story in *Les Corbeaux* by Becque of a shady character who was called Duhamel. I say *was* called, because when the play was put on recently the actors at the Comédie française had the charming thought of changing the name of this character to spare my feelings. It was not a major character—only a passing reference—and they rightly supposed that a name, even a widely distributed one, although it cannot be monopolized, will yet have taken color from the personality of a living person, and in that sense be detached from its public quality, or, if I might put it so, from its natural anonymity. To clear my thoughts let me extend the discussion outside my own case. The name of Claudel, for example, is invested with so clear and so luminous a significance that it would certainly be unwise, quite apart from any question of taste or manners, to use this old French name for a character in a play or in a story. By so doing one would run the risk of distracting the attention of the reader and evoking strong mental images in his mind from which he would be unable to free himself.

The secret is, for the conscientious story-teller, to persuade his character to agree from the outset that he may have to change his name. I realize that this is by no means easy; the heroes of novels are not the men to be bullied; and that is why I cautiously write "persuade his character." It is a case for persuasion.

A more than usually indiscreet inquirer asked me lately how I chose the names of my characters. "Oh," I said, "I don't choose them—they present themselves and tell me their names." Of course, some of them take their time over the process, just as in real life. There is a man whom I meet every year at a friend's house and still I do not know his name. We know each other really well, this man and I, and we enjoy our talks. Have we never been introduced? Was I thinking of something else at the time? Have I simply forgotten the name? I really do not know, but next time I meet him I will ask him his name if I remember to do so and if it seems to be the right thing to do at the moment. It is the same in the kingdom of dreams. We discover our characters and get to know them, then one day they whisper their name, or shout it, or mumble it, and there is nothing left for us but to accept it. Sometimes we are surprised, sometimes sorry, sometimes delighted; and we may even say, ironically, like Hugo to his heckler, "I hardly hoped for so much!"

To change the name of a hero is a ticklish undertaking, and one which may fail in the sense that it may falsify the interplay of the characters and hold up the narrative.

I remember a good book, well written and well put together, where the author at the last minute re-christened his principal character in the final proof corrections. This serious operation had been too hastily carried out, or, more precisely, badly done. Unnoticed by the corrector the original name remained, preposterous and inexplicable, here and there in the folds of the story. The result for the reader was a feeling of discomfort, fraud, uncertainty, and, above all, unreality. The life of creatures of the imagination is often more intense in the moral sphere than that of creatures of flesh and blood, but it is a magical life with secret rigid laws against which we may not transgress. One little mistake of this kind and the ghosts vanish into thin air.

Earlier in this book I deplored the fact that magistrates should take so much notice of irate plaintiffs who instinctively recognize themselves in every caricature. I am afraid that in disputes about names, too, the courts seldom have the sense to dismiss the charges.

Writers of today, conforming to the exacting demands of realism, have abandoned purely conventional names for their characters. It would be anachronistic and decidedly precious nowadays to use names such as Matamore, Léandre, Scapin, or Zerbinette for the heroes of a story that takes place in sight of the Eiffel Tower, between Montmartre and Montrouge. Names must be real and living, the direct utterance of the people itself, rooted in the daily life of the nation and the language.

We must have freedom and fresh air, and a just and broad liberty that is directed against no particular individual and can shock no one. As I have suggested, if an author is so minded as to call his characters Honegger, Herriot, or Giraudoux, then he is making a mistake and laying himself open to ridicule. The whole question can really be left safely to public opinion.

I believe there are two Goriots in the telephone directory, one Raquin, two Grandets, a dozen Vautrins, six or seven Bergerets, about four Pons, and in default of a single Pécuchet about eight Bouvards. Should we offer these good people a decoration for tolerance and self-denial on the ground that they have not yet, with the consent of the judges, thrown the most glorious treasures of our libraries into the fire?

XVIII

THE MYSTERY OF TALENT

WORDS are the property of a whole nation, one of the safest and least disputed of its treasures. Let him who wishes help himself, let him who dares employ them! They are there, like the air they need for their own life of sound.

A man seizes a word that is common property and instantly he makes it his personal property. By his way of pronouncing it, by the play of his muscles and the depth of his breathing, by his delivery, his tone of voice, his accent, and even by such subsidiary factors as the movements of his face, the expression of his eyes, the gestures of his hands and limbs and body, the man who says a single word marks it at once with his own imprint. He betrays his habits, his appetites, his passions, his failings, his regrets, and his sorrows. He says the little word *vin,* and we know at once whether he likes wine or is afraid of it, whether he is thirsty or not, whether he is a connoisseur or a barbarian. He says the word *amour,* and by the way he pronounces these two syllables he disturbs us, or moves us, or annoys us, or makes us laugh. A word which is common property has become the word, the property, the symbol of a particular man.

Printing seems to be tending to make words lose this evanescent and private quality and to label them with their enduring and general meaning. It seems so, but it is not certain. For a sensitive reader each word changes its quality and its resonance and perhaps its meaning according to whether it is used by a poet or a prose-writer, a master or an apprentice, a shy man or an aggressive one, a soft-hearted man or a hard one. The qualities of style play a large part, but they are not the only cause. Very few writers can make me feel hungry. They can conjure up all sorts of food and drink, describe venison and cold meats and pastries, juicy fruits, savory sauces, but they very rarely have the power to put my digestive apparatus in motion and stimulate my glands. Dickens on the other hand is marvelous at this. He writes "A frugal meal," and I do not know why but my mouth begins to water. He does not need to resort to any artifice; he has the gift, and his words, even when they are chilled by translation and typography, assume a tempting flavor. He writes "Ham, beer, rounds of toast," just that, and really it all seems delicious. The identical words written by some gloomy and dyspeptic author would fill me with disgust.

Colette, with whom I have had the pleasure of lunching and dining many times, certainly never appeared to be a gourmand. She likes good food and when she takes it she gives it her enlightened attention. When she pronounces the names of foods in my presence she does not stimulate my imagination particularly; but when she writes in the simplest possible way such words as "white bread, tomato, garlic, olive oil," I am hungry at once.

It is quite incomprehensible, but it is a fact. The same word printed by Colette or by Giraudoux has not at all the same flavor. It is as if it were served with a different sauce. Sensuality is a gift, and it is a many-sided gift.

It is not given to every writer to be obscene. There must be natural innocence, or, better still, frankness. Onesimus had the most startling successes, they say, in his love affairs. He had only to show himself and women would fall on their knees. He was really only a sort of specialist, a virtuoso and an acrobat. He writes freely about his affairs in an exceedingly daring way. His books are without merit, at any rate, in this respect. They would make even love-sick youths and intemperate old men yawn with boredom. The words of libertinism lose all their color and all their glow in passing through his pen. Onesimus will never be anything but a dull author and a lukewarm libertine.

Eusebius is a very gifted writer. One day he decided that he would be a great love poet; by which he meant a poet of carnal love. Immediately he set to work. He raised a monument, no less, an ithyphallic monument to the goddess of voluptuousness. His pictures are completely unlicensed and brilliantly painted. The curious thing is that nobody is stirred by them. They are curiously cold and didactic—a sort of academic gallantry. One has the impression of reading a text-book for libertines, or perhaps a "course in eroticism for higher forms." Any young widow who happened on these disturbing works would end by falling into a dreamless and peaceful slumber. No; sensuality cannot be evoked at will. Emma Bovary, on the other hand, is a shameless creature. The laces of her corset will long hiss in the ears of lustful magistrates.

Balzac can move our imagination with a few strokes of the pen. "Vénus tout entière"? Actually that would be too much for anyone. Diane de Maufrigneuse is dressing hurriedly; one glimpses her white body for a second through the transparent veil of her linen. The lady does up "her lucky bodice, the one that does up in front"—and Amélie Camusot, who is helping her to put on her stockings, suddenly kisses her knee in an impulse of admiration. The picture is stealthy and perfect. It dwells in the mind much longer than a whole scientific treatise about love and passion.

Only talent can give words their living power and meaning. And talent is a very mysterious thing. Mauriac, when he likes, can paint to perfection the blazing sun of his native Gascony. It is a frightening sunlight. When we encounter it we suddenly feel the sweat breaking out on our forehead. It is indeed a sun of suffering, designed to illuminate our darkness and reveal our unhappiness to ourselves. Mauriac may write no more than "It was a fine day." I smell the odor of the pines, the sweet smell of fields and lilac, but something clutches at my throat. The blue heavens are turbid and tragic. What can the light of the sun do against the darkness of man?

Thus we rack our brains, bullied by our own talents. If we try to frustrate them, or dominate them, or conquer them we only impoverish ourselves. Yet if we accept them without argument we become their slaves.

There is no rule except perhaps this simple old-fashioned one: never pretend to be something that you are not.

That may appear to be an easy maxim to follow, but it is not so easy as it looks.

PART III

NOTES ON THE ART
OF NARRATION

NOTES ON THE ART OF NARRATION

CRITICS can easily distinguish a dozen varieties of fiction, but for my part I can only see two; one is the novel that makes us forget life, the other is the novel that explains our life to us. I am careful not to say that one variety is either better or worse than the other. *Dominique* is a splendid story and a fine example of its kind; *Treasure Island,* on the other hand, is an amazing book which ought to have a place in every library.

According to the authorities the adjective *romanesque* can be applied to people or things which appertain to the novel, and thus take on a wonderful or fabulous character. The noun *roman* has a corresponding connotation.

Being the natural successor in popular esteem to the epic poem, the novel sets out to satisfy a need that is very natural, and very keen, a need for the extraordinary.

It may seem that the word *romanesque,* thus defined, makes an uneasy partnership with the word *familier.* How can what is familiar to us be wonderful? Yet that is the miracle; the *romanesque familier* suddenly makes us aware of the extraordinary within the ordinary, the exceptional underneath the daily round.

Man needs to be diverted, and distracted in the Pascalian sense of the word, by stories and representations of things that can hold his interest and offer him enchantment and forgetfulness, a sort of intoxication. The epic poem, the stage, the novel, and nowadays the cinema, have successively made an effort to respond to this need.

The epic poem is not dead in eastern countries. It still plays its Homeric role very effectively. In order to excite interest and work its magic it relies chiefly on music and rhythmic artifices. In addition it occupies itself with extraordinary occurrences, such as are likely to strike the slowest and dullest imagination. The novel, in its early days, did nothing more. The tale of chivalry, for example, with which it seems that Miguel de Cervantes broke several lances, was first and foremost a story of extraordinary and probably miraculous happenings. Monsters, giants, wizards, are the familiar heroes of those narrative poems which we read purely for entertainment and which were not intended by their authors to make any contribution to knowledge of the human mind.

In spite of the realistic revolution this tradition is far from being obsolete. Apart from juvenile literature there is a whole range of novels which depend on fairy story. The adventure novel, a certain sort of historical novel, the cloak and sword romance, the prophetic novel in the style of Wells, the scientific or pseudo-scientific novel in the style of Jules Verne, all these are descendants of the old romance.

The tradition is not dead, but it has been very much weakened by the successes of the realistic novel and the experiments that occupied the whole of the nineteenth century. These experiments represent an important page in the history of literature, and notable acquisitions in the psychological sphere have been derived from what may be termed the realistic revolution. Only the excesses of realism have been able to hinder its progress. Many writers have been under the impression that in order to sustain interest, to replace the miraculous, and to make their readers forget the enchanters and the gallant deeds and the exploits of chivalry, they must ransack reality for surprising and horrible things. This accounts for the violence of naturalism, its brutal writing and its verbal excesses. These sallies are not forgotten, and perhaps they are not yet finished; I do not disapprove of them, for they have been instructive.

The *romanesque familier,* the novel of everyday life, has emerged from all these experiments. Novelists have at last realized that in order to arouse and sustain the attention of their readers it was not necessary to drag in magicians or fairies, that the picture of reality was capable of attracting the reader, that this picture need not include that new form of unreality which the brutalities of naturalism have developed, that the main thing, in fact, was to demonstrate what we look at every day without seeing it, the really wonderful material which forms the texture of our daily life, and thus to add something essential to our mental picture of mankind. To embrace this formula I propose the modest expression, the *romanesque familier.*

The novel of everyday life, profiting by the experiences of realism and naturalism, has evolved certain rules and defined certain practices. The influence of environment, which has been a determining factor for half a century in our fiction, maintains its importance; that goes without saying; but the art of story-telling has changed greatly, and the modern novelist has abandoned those descriptions of forty and fifty pages which our masters of the preceding generation thought necessary. No one disputes the importance of the idea of heredity which the naturalists made such a fuss of—it still dominates our works without overloading them. That this principle has become excessive in the art of the novel may be demonstrated by one simple observation: I know less about the past history of my friends and my children and my wife and myself than is usually given by the naturalistic novelists when they introduce one of their minor characters. A sense of proportion is a necessity in the construction of the modern novel.

But there is one question the modern novelist ought to ask himself as a matter of discipline, a very troublesome question which he must put to himself frequently and firmly, the question of subject.

The word "subject" is one of those many words which in French are capable of having a great number of different meanings. It is difficult to define such words, for their etymological meaning is often quite narrow. They express at once too much and too little. All the same when we speak of the subject of a work of music, or painting, or sculture, or poetry, we know very well what we mean. We refer freely to the subject of an opera, or of a poem, or of a picture. If we try to arrive at an exact definition we encounter difficulties. And it is no solution to amalgamate the word "subject" with the word "object" (which is by no means the same thing), or to substitute such words as "theme" or "motive" (the last named is applicable, for example, to plastic or static work like statuary or painting). Moreover the word "subject" ought to be used with some restraint. "The Rape of the Sabine Women" is a subject picture; the portrait of Mme. Chalgrin is not, because the painter has taken a model, and was not occupied with what one might call a subject. There is a subject in *L'Apprenti Sorcier* by Paul Dukas, and also in the *Pastoral Symphony;* but there is no subject in this sense in Bach's double concerto. A still-life by Chardin usually has no subject.

By subject, therefore, I mean an historic or legendary event, a philosophic idea, a moral argument, sometimes simply a combination of anecdotal elements which may serve as the foundation or impulse of a work of art. As the word suggests, a subject is thus precisely something which lies underneath appearance, the essential reality which determines and co-ordinates the outer aspects.

A subject is indispensable for certain sorts of literary work, and is merely tolerated by others. There are some which ought to avoid a subject, and when a philosophical story is written to a thesis it is liable to take the color of a moral tract. The short story may be sometimes a picture, sometimes a portrait, sometimes a subject work. Poems can support a subject, but may easily be the worse for it. In the case of a full-length novel the subject is a matter of primary importance and needs to be examined in broad daylight.

One can easily guess the origin of some of the best

stories; the author has had an idea, and round this idea
he has built his work so as to exploit it to full effect.
La Peau de chagrin is a model for works of this kind.
Everyone in the world knows the subject of this book.
A man comes into the possession of a wild ass's skin
which is invested with magical powers; every time the
man expresses a wish his wish is satisfied, but the skin
shrinks a little. Soon the owner of the skin runs through
the gamut of his desires. The moral emerges clearly
from this story and it is hardly necessary to add that
La Peau de chagrin is rather a philosophical fable than
a work of fiction. Balzac's genius was big enough to
allow him to indulge in diversions of all descriptions.

The Picture of Dorian Grey is a work of the same
kind. Let me remind you in a few words, from memory,
of the subject of the story. A good-looking young man,
with every gift, has his portrait drawn by a painter.
The young man commits faults, or, more precisely, sins.
He remains wonderfully good-looking, but every time
he commits a fault some sign of ugliness or evil appears
on the portrait, which is kept carefully hidden. The
day that, after a long life, he seizes the implacable
picture furiously in order to destroy it, he falls as if
struck by lightning. He is discovered disfigured by all
the ugliness of his life lying in front of a portrait that
is still as young and radiant as when it was first painted.
It is only necessary to recount this anecdote, stripped of
all its beauty of style, to show that Wilde's story is at
the same time a philosophical story and a moral one,
or even, if I dare suggest it, a moralizing one.

Voltaire's *Candide* is a perfect work, which would be
enough to make the fame of any writer. This little

novel is not a novel, it is a philosophical story, and moreover a model of its kind.

I am quoting a few works at random as examples of what I mean, and it is unnecessary to mention many. Side by side with the works that are classified as novels, yet are, properly speaking, philosophical stories, can be placed a number of other stories which satisfy the ordinary definition of a novel but are really simply good pictures of character or manners and are really trying to propound a "subject," that is to say, to develop a thesis or prove something. This is the case with many of the novelists of the naturalistic school, for example, with several of Émile Zola's works.

It is worthy of note that subject-stories are easy to read or to summarize. The underlying design of the author is apparent throughout the work. The philosophy behind the story, when it is not being expounded by the author himself, is entrusted to one of those characters who explain what is going on behind the scenes. The novel reader, if he wants to summarize such a work, can say at once: "It's about a man in such and such a situation who finds himself forced into such and such a line of conduct, with the result that..." and so on.

The danger of a subject, when it is not in the hands of a great master and when it does not turn openly into a moral tale, is that the characters may become subordinated to the subject. The writer is then left with a sort of algebraic operation. A situation is given which implies certain consequences and the characters are forced, whether they like it or not, to go through this mill. If the novelist is a great artist and in love with his subject he can find a way out; and his characters, even when they are subjugated—I ought to say "subjected"—to the laws of this type of work, take on a life of their own. But usually they suffer for it, or perhaps I ought to say that truth suffers, owing to the conflict between the needs of the argument and the necessities of the characters. The plot is worked out, but at the risk of extinguishing the actors.

I was listening one day to a story that was being read to me aloud. The theme had interested me originally, but as the reading went on I felt my interest evaporate little by little. Originally I had said, "What a fine subject!" yet as one episode yielded to another the book seemed to me to be arbitrary and divorced from life, in fact, unreal and tiresome. I was trying to discover the reasons for my dislike when suddenly they forced themselves on my notice: it was "a fine subject," perfectly handled. Every chapter seemed to be like the proof of a theorem, and I found myself awaiting, from one line to the next, the final implacable Q.E.D.

The words "idealist" and "ideology" have become distinctly depreciated in our time and people contrast them scornfully with words such as "realist" and "realism." This is too simple a view. It must still be borne in mind that the great danger of ideas is that they may encourage us to escape from reality, to lose the sense of it.

I know well enough that the novelist should not take up an extreme position and renounce "subject" altogether—there are certain sorts of novel where a subject is a necessity, and subjects have been responsible for many of the great masterpieces—but I believe that the novel is distinguished from the moral or philosophical story in that it has no subject. The novel is essentially a portrait or a portrait gallery. The portraits are not immobile; they take part in the action, and the action or rather actions that they take are not directed towards an ideological proof. The characters of fiction, when they are really alive, create their own action and determine their own situations. If these events happen to prove something or depict something, that is an added meaning which was not part of the novelist's plan. The true novel has no moral to point, and is almost always difficult to explain or to summarize, and difficult to understand, like life itself. When I see the critics in difficulties about giving an account of a book, my interest is immediately awakened. For life, life which is our model, is difficult to account for.

It needs self-denial to forgo a subject when one is writing a novel. How often I hear estimable story-tellers trying to explain their work! One says: "It's all about the problem of monism and dualism, more or less...." Another announces: "It's the dispute between East and West presented in the form of a novel...." Some authors think, while writing a story that is otherwise excellent, that they are "treating the post-War problem" or "dealing with the serious question of paternal responsibility...." There are very few who will say simply, "It's the story of a man," or "It's the story of a woman," or "It's the story of a family." Often the very best among them yield to the allure of ideology; instead of saying "It's the story of a man and a woman," they say: "It's the story of Man and Woman."

I admire ambition, especially the sort of ambition that is realized in work done, and I believe that we must keep promises we have not even made.

The difficult thing is to resist the curiosity of the inquisitive. Sometimes, tired of leaving questions unanswered, I give in and explain my own books; I speak of problems, and great questions, and processes, and master ideas, etc. I am extremely grateful to the people who do not force me to make these speeches for my own defense.

A character is not fully formed from the moment of its conception. It may become so. A sublime innocence goes to the making of a typical character. The good novelist does not deliberately set out to depict the average Frenchman at the beginning of the twentieth century—he just portrays an ordinary man. He may find later that this man is extraordinarily typical of the average Frenchman at the beginning of the twentieth century, and he may even discover, in rare cases, that this character stands for "man" pure and simple, the man of all time and all nations. Such portraits cannot be made to order.

A representative character is the unconscious work of a great artist in the first place; later he may become the work of a whole people, of a race, of a world, because the whole world may involuntarily imitate this character, even if he is ridiculous, even if he is sublime.

The creation of a representative character leads to an ideology after the event, possibly on the author's part, inevitably on the part of others. Three centuries of criticism have poured into the bowl of *Hamlet* more ideas and systems and doctrines than Shakespeare could have imagined himself.

In spite of history, the great creator of new facts, the available "subjects" are not unlimited. Lists have been drawn up of the possible dramatic situations, and even the poetical themes can be enumerated. The great novel "subjects" can be similarly classified, and each generation takes them up again, exploits them, and finally exhausts them. It would be better to abandon them once and for all, or to reduce them to a minor status without architectural significance. The novel of every-day life is better without a subject because it is then free from preconception; that is at once its merit and its danger; for if it does not imitate the logic of life it cannot fall back on the earlier logic of the moral fables.

When a novelist exploits a subject he usually tries to extract all the marrow from it. He pursues his idea right to the end, even when perseverance will lead him to absurdity and improbability. Intercourse with ideas is apt to go to the head. If Flaubert had finished *Bouvard et Pécuchet,* the plot of which we know, he would have given the world a systematic work. Death had pity on him.

There is nothing more attractive than a subject-story when it first comes into its author's mind. It appears to him then like a piece of furniture, ready and in position, and all he has to do is to fill the drawers. When the subject becomes too obvious through the texture of the work, he adds a conventional disguise. Any subject, even the best and the newest, contains the germ of conventionality.

Accustomed as they are to trying to impress the public with high-sounding formulae and hollow phrases, the politicians boast freely that they follow their opinions logically to the limit. They are quite wrong. A good surgeon, for example, does not always go to the limit. He is working in living flesh, and he knows that he is responsible; and he knows when to stop or to change his method of approach or to turn back.

The true novelist may sometimes pursue his characters to the end of their lives; but he would not think of pursuing his ideas to the bitter end, nor those of anyone else.

To be a slave to an idea is not really slavery, it is a form of indulgence. But art thrives under restraint and is killed by indulgence.

Even when it is discharged from theorizing and "subjects" and pretentiousness, the art of story-telling is still hedged round with restrictions and difficulties. Every novelist must reach once a day the limits of his power, and this critical encounter does not often happen to take place when he is in his study with white paper in front of him. The material must have been sorted out long before the actual writing is done. Usually it is in daily life that we measure our strength and our weakness. Sometimes I hear men and women talking, in a crowd, in a train, or during a meal, and I realize that I am noticing a trait of character, happening on a friendship, overhearing a secret; but at that actual moment I am quite incapable of transcribing these discoveries into words. Later, much later, I may, perhaps, be able to give out again what I have seen, but for the moment I cannot. Yet even if I do not succeed I know that someone else will, and that he, informed by our experiences and guided by his own genius, will put into words things of which we have merely had a glimpse.

The artists of the past have been great men and their works overawe us. But it would be wrong to suppose that they have said everything, and that we have come on the scene too late. It is never too late; the portrait of man will never be finished. Lucky is he who can add one feature, one single touch. Jules Renard, a minor master, has observed and fixed some aspects which Balzac, the colossus, may never have suspected. Methods improve and adapt themselves to new conditions. Real life is inexhaustible.

I know what I would like to do and I cannot always do it. I know what I ought not to do, and I cannot always not do it.

Real life is inexhaustible; that does not mean that it is easy to grasp.

Much nonsense has been talked about what is often called photographic truth.

Actually nothing is more capricious, more human, and more unreliable than the camera. Sometimes the most modest apparatus is positively lyrical; at other times it is dull and idiotic; at other times it sees nothing at all. Generally speaking, I think that photography today has an alarming tendency to improve on nature, and possibly on man as well. I do not dislike photography but I am seldom inclined to accept it as evidence. Photography is an interpreter.

What is incorrectly called photographic truth is actu-

ally a vulgar and coarse reality that is easily accessible—
a reality in fact that is not interpreted, or only summarily so.

We cannot use the word reality in a discussion of
the spirit of the novel without reviving a host of ancient
quarrels. The most important of these is the one about
the truth of dialogue.

If I were asked to name a work which is notable for
the realism of its pictures and of its conversation, I
should, perhaps, say *Le Neveu de Rameau*. Even the
character of Rameau's nephew, the one whom Diderot
calls *Lui,* never misses a chance of self-criticism. He
says: "I am a fool, an ignoramus, a waster..."; but this
ignoramus, referring to the clumsiness of his fingers on
the piano, expresses himself as follows: "In spite of
what they are, these damn things have had to get into
line and get used to finding their way about the notes
and flying over the keys."

Yet *Le Neveu de Rameau* is a masterpiece, a model
of living realism. One would not alter a single line.

This example, in my opinion, settles the question of
so-called photographic truth in the dialogue of novels.
I am ready to believe that in the eighteenth century
everyone wrote and spoke correctly; I am still more
ready to believe that it is puerile to insist on reproduc-
ing the turns of phrase and inaccuracies of current
speech in the dialogue of a book.

The skill of a writer consists in enshrining individual
or local peculiarities by incorporating them in the genius
of the language. This implies that the genius of the
language, that is to say the deeper meaning of the language, should be respected even in a realistic dialogue.

True realism is to be found in thoughts rather than in words.

Any novelist of the twentieth century who is not utterly ungrateful should bless the name of Émile Zola. This man of genius, unjustly disparaged by people who have never read him, has done a thankless piece of work on our behalf. I do not refer only to the great classification of the social categories; I am thinking of Zola's courageous attempts towards realism of language, and at the same time of his passion for describing everything, saying everything, throwing on everything a blinding light, a light which seems to expose mystery itself.

Another dispute, much less thrashed out, concerns the realism of thoughts, by which I mean the possibility of such and such a character, given his environment, really thinking the thoughts we attribute to him.

After much trouble we are at last beginning to triumph over ignorant criticism. Only lately a well-meaning reader volunteered the remark, "You describe an office employee. Right. Are you sure an office employee could have ideas such as you credit him with?"

If there is such a thing as foolish realism it is of a sort which vitiates public judgment and gives rise to questions of this kind.

So I describe an office employee and I attribute certain thoughts to him. The important thing is not that he has actually thought these thoughts; it is that in exposing these thoughts he identifies them. The important thing is that the novelist gives form and life to those obscure thoughts with which so many minds are concerned.

All men suffer, even the most simple—and perhaps they more than the others—not from not having ideas, but from experiencing them incompletely. Men suffer from not knowing how to crystallize their secret thoughts in words, the very ones that are most vital to them, and the novelist would be failing in his duty if, in portraying character, he were to limit himself to the obvious thoughts which everyone formulates. He must throw open the gates with a daring gesture and tear aside the veil.

People who ask the question quoted above usually go on more or less as follows: "I am a lawyer, or I am a manager, and, of course, I might think of such things ...but an office employee! You astound me!" I am always amused by the *naïveté* and vanity of this objection. The important thing is that an idea thus brought to the light of day shall be recognized and accepted.

As far as I myself am concerned in this academic dispute, I have summarized my opinion in two lines. At the beginning of a story *(Deux Hommes)* I imagine the thoughts of a man walking. I complete the picture by these words: "Il pensait à toutes ces choses et à mille autres encore, mais il ne savait pas qu'il y pensait."

If I cannot help men to know what they are thinking about, what use am I in this world?

In France the rules of classical art prohibit a mixture of genre; tragedy and comedy must always be separated on the stage. To the novel this rule is inapplicable. Possibly some works demand a uniform light—there are stories which are purely dramatic and others which are purely burlesque. The true novel, like life, is a complex of darkness and light. I can hardly imagine a great work of fiction without humor. Some stories of a historical character, such as *Salammbô,* can dispense with humor, but how can anyone who describes his fellow-men renounce this precious adjunct? Balzac has a violent, sometimes coarse, sense of humor, which is marvelously suited to his vast narrative ambitions. If there were no such word as humor it would have to be coined for Dickens. Stendhal's humor is a great part of his genius. Dostoevsky mixes admirably the colors of tragedy with the Slavonic humor of which he has given perfect examples in his novels.

Hardy is a great novelist apparently devoid of humor, but his work is bathed in poetry. When poetry and humor are both lacking nothing can replace them. Galsworthy is a good writer and an honest painter of a society, but he lacks humor, and his work is rarely touched with poetry.

Paul Bourget displays neither humor nor poetry in the portrayal of feelings and passions. His psychology was essentially didactic.

The English word "humor" has supplanted our old word "humeur," which incidentally has many different meanings. Let us adopt "humor" deliberately and try to define it. Humor is different from the truly comic— the primary aim of the latter is to raise a laugh and it has a style and a language of its own; humor is also different from simple gaiety, which is a more or less fleeting state of mind, and is not revealing from the psychological point of view. Humor consists of certain lights and shades which display an object under different aspects, some of which may be contradictory and by this very fact revelatory. In humor there is a natural reserve and a continence which are not apparent in the frankly comic. When it is systematically applied humor is very likely to miss its mark—it should be used only when circumstances demand it. The comic is determined to laugh from the word "go," but humor does not always laugh, and when it does it is because it cannot help it.

Humor is the natural state of mind of a person who has not given up hope of understanding everything he sees and almost everything he knows.

A dispute has been raging recently on the subject of the language of the novelists. Some hold that the style should be highly polished in accordance with artistic rules, others take the view that the aim of the novel is to create living characters and that style of writing is a secondary concern.

I think I understand the reason for this misunderstanding. The so-called "artistic style," honored by the Goncourts, has done great harm to prose narrative by removing it from nature and loading it with jewels.

If you want an example open *Madame Gervaisais* and read: "There she sat, charmingly tired of supporting the graceful line of her figure, her sloping shoulders, her slender neck, and with the suspicion of a smile on her face she listened, lightly indifferent to the snatches of gossip of the little groups around her, who were seated on chairs covered with tapestry depicting the theological virtues." In that passage you can find the principle underlying the dispute to which I am referring.

This dispute is not dead. Many good writers still think that, since their aim is to lift us out of ourselves into the stream of their events and to associate us for an hour or two with the fate of their fictitious characters, there is danger in lingering to enjoy points of detail.

The solution to the problem is probably quite simple. Certainly the story must lift the reader out of himself, "ravish" him in the original sense of the word —that is an absolute rule. But in addition each page should be good enough in itself to justify a less cursory reading. This rule is founded in history, offered to us by the great masterpieces. Re-read the opening of *Le Père Goriot,* the end of *Le Rouge et le Noir,* any chapter of *Madame Bovary,* re-read *Don Quixote,* and there will be no need of further argument.

I ask a good language, a healthy language, clear and strong and vital. I ask also a musical language. Just because the novel of everyday life forbids lyrical expression and showy realism, because it clings to the only true reality, that of the soul, such a story to be appreciated and to hold the attention of the reader must have recourse to the persuasion of music, to the play of sound which has so great a power over our mind and our senses. How can anyone say that the style of a novel is of minor importance? There are some authors whom we never read simply because their personal musical rhythm is not in accord with our own.

Saint-Saëns wrote: "It is impossible to speak without singing, either in verse or prose. As soon as you raise your voice, as soon as you are excited, you declaim, and, without your suspecting it, you improvise a recitative mixed with snatches of melody."

So much for the music of language. How about ideas?

Music accompanies all my thoughts. Reading, even writing, I can hum tunes if they happen to fit in with the rhythm of my thoughts. I select these melodies instinctively and I abandon them when they are no longer in unison with my inner music. But it is rare for such a counterpoint to be the result of chance. Only rarely, for example, do I hear music played while I am reading or writing without suffering discordance.

I feel that the music of style is an essential condition of its spiritual influence. A good novelist is in the first place a man who knows some of life's secrets; he must also be a man who, in saying what he has to say, produces naturally a verbal music which is his signature and the private mark of his genius.

I hardly like to give advice to young writers who consult me in these matters, but sometimes, in my anxiety to help them, I may say, "In the opening pages of your works the melody must not falter. The reader must be carried away without shock or friction. He does not yet know your people, and he is not yet interested in the story or captured by the strength of the descriptions and the verisimilitude of the characters. So let the music of style help him over the early stages of the journey. Sing well to seduce the heart you hope to conquer."

I pleaded above for a healthy language. Some sophisticated readers have a weakness for peculiarities of language and construction. They think wrongly that a writer is original because of his turns of phrase or his vocabulary. True originality is not a matter of form, especially among prose writers—it is a quality of the mind. These perverted readers remind me of jaded gourmets who dream of extraordinary foods and want to eat swallows' nests and tapirs' trunks and sharks' fins. Idle fancies of an hour. The eccentricities of style are nothing. The only thing that matters, I repeat, is that ineffable music which is the song of the soul.

Pascal has said: "There are some people who would wish an author never to speak of those subjects of which others have spoken; if he does so they accuse him of saying nothing new.... They might as well accuse him of using old words: as if the same thoughts, differently used, did not form new subject-matter, just in the same way as the same words arranged differently form different ideas."

In my view this admirable paragraph settles all possible disputes about technique and true originality.

I might add that the masters whose originality is expressed by peculiarity of form can easily be imitated, parrot-like; it is difficult to imitate deep originality, which belongs to the very substance of being.

A good language, I repeat, a clear language, and that means a language that is simple and correct. A pure language, not one that is mummified by purism. Some purists jeer at good writers for mistakes which may well be deliberate. When an author of experience and talent allows himself to write "par contre" or "partir à Paris" I shut my eyes and assent. He must have some reason for making such a mistake. Paul Claudel, great poet and etymologist, has made some pertinent remarks on this subject.

Only one thing really matters in evaluating the professional story-writers. If they teach us something about man, that is to say, something about ourselves, then we can offer them our unstinted gratitude; if they do no such thing, then the least they can do is to entertain us and make us forget that while giving us nothing they have taken something from us.

PART IV

THE CHURCH
OF FRENCH LITERATURE

I

THE CLASSICAL TRADITION

In a page at once friendly and treacherous that he wrote for the *Liber amicorum Romain Rolland,* Georg Brandes said, just before he died: "J'aime mieux les livres qui perdent beaucoup, s'ils sont traduits." I quote this phrase of Brandes's word for word because it seems to be designed to prove that there is something untranslatable in every human idiom. Brandes was a great scholar. He understood and spoke several languages, and the opinion he expresses above is obviously colored with egoism; it is the opinion of a dilettante of the mind. Every language has its esoteric rites and every literature its inner temple and only those who can give the pass-word may enter the holy of holies.

The literary output of a nation or of a man comprises one part which is universally assimilable. Given a good translation such work enters into the consciousness of other nations and may even take a place of honor there. The masterpieces of Swift and Daniel Defoe immediately took their proper rank in the French libraries, and moreover they came to our notice at a time when everybody in France wrote well and when anonymous translations were frequently models of style and good taste.

French literature is certainly rich in works which can easily be translated. It is not, however, through the medium of translations that it has made its way in the world and won its true glory. I once saw Molière's *Avare* played by an old Finnish actor in a theater in Helsingfors. Disguised in the strange and beautiful dialect of Väinämöinen, Molière was still Molière; but one could feel that part of his unique genius stayed in the filter, as the chemists say, and that some of the qualities of this famous work are inseparable from the mother tongue.

It has been the remarkable destiny of French literature to win the attention of the civilized world, not only by offering it works of universal appeal but by converting it to the beauty of the original language. The educated world likes to read French literature in French. Great men of genius like Tolstoy and Dostoevsky have spoken for the whole world without teaching Russian to many of their readers; on the other hand, I am sure that many foreigners have learned French conscientiously so as to be able to read our writers in the original text. French is not used much for commercial purposes and the man who wants to travel and handle big business had better learn English or German; both these languages, for material reasons, have extended their influence, and from this extension the writers, or rather their ideals, have benefited. With us it is quite different. Foreigners of all countries learn French so as to be able to share the spiritual treasures of France rather than for utilitarian reasons. Molière, Balzac, and Anatole France throw open doors through which our business men find excellent opportunities; for which service I must admit they show neither surprise nor gratitude.

This state of affairs is worth examination. It is not enough to say that French is extremely rich and varied; in addition it brings a message to the world, and we must consider the origin and the nature of this message.

Of all the remarkable phenomena which it is given to us of the twentieth century to witness the most striking is undoubtedly the standardization of civilization. This phenomenon, which arises from improved facilities for intercourse between peoples and races, is now in rapid development. We cannot foresee all the consequences but we know very well that in a comparatively few years, with certain reserves owing to differing climatic conditions, there will be only one solitary system of civilization, monotonous and indistinctive, left on earth.

Until the time of the great colonial fever and the industrial revolution of the last century, in spite of travelers' tales and business enterprise, the world was ruled by diverse systems of civilization which would have no truck with one another and which guarded their treasures and their secrets jealously. There seemed to be no possibility of real fusion or compromise or alliance between the Asiatic civilizations and the so-called European or western civilization.

Western-thinking men knew very well that the Asiatic civilizations were not to be despised, but they had many reasons for admiring the western civilization which was their own, and in which, through over six thousand years of history, several distinct primitive social ideas were incorporated. Egypt, the countries of the Levant, Greece, Italy, and North Africa had each evolved different and at first opposing civilizations which were finally united in one civilization that might be called Mediterranean and was thenceforward associated with Europe as a whole, a continent fertile in genius.

Although I have tried to do so all my life it is difficult to distinguish between the spiritual and the material in this civilization. It can be said, however, that for sixty centuries a spiritual treasure has been accumulating in that part of the world whose shores are washed by the Mediterranean, the Atlantic Ocean, and the North Sea, and that this treasure consists not only of works of art and literature, but, more important still, of intellectual methods and moral traditions, in fact, of metaphysical and religious doctrines.

Naturally this gradual and prodigious human experience has not been gained without setbacks and loss of continuity. But during the most troubled periods of history there have always been scholars to rescue the essence of our precious heritage, to recopy and annotate famous writings, to restore or corroborate intellectual traditions.

I know some distinguished thinkers who regard the French Renaissance as a disastrous event without which, according to them, we should have seen the development of a truly original culture in France. Brilliant though this paradox may be, it distracts us from our magnificent achievements only to surrender us to vain regrets for a hardly discernible shadow. The great French writers and poets before the Renaissance were all, or nearly all, saturated in Greek and Roman culture. Far from making us deplore the Renaissance in retrospect, they herald it and show it as a necessity that would not be denied.

Just as at certain moments of their history groups of human beings have shown their strong desire of forming a nation, so towards the middle of the sixteenth century the French writers and poets gave vigorous expression to their desire to form a literature, and to begin by codifying their language. They suddenly decided to revive the Mediterranean tradition, to reclaim their heritage from a rich and ancient civilization, the only one known to them, and to propagate that civilization throughout a whole nation.

Yes, the most remarkable event of the sixteenth century in France was this spiritual resolution to revive a tradition, not by the complete abandonment of all the original characteristics of a group of human beings but by the submission of those characteristics to an illustrious ancient discipline. In just such a way, in some families, one may see a son renounce his own original plans in order to devote himself to his father's business and maintain the good name and fortune of the house.

To tell the truth, everything tended to urge France to this succession. Among the peoples called Latin for the reason that they were longer than others under the yoke of the Roman conquest, France occupies a unique geographic situation; she is closely hedged in by Anglo-Saxon and Germanic peoples, and, in spite of foreign invasions, she has always resisted Germanization. In giving evidence of her intention to remain Mediterranean by culture, and in affirming her inheritance of Greek and Latin civilization, she gave a fundamentally moral force to her resistance. Moreover she discovered political autonomy earlier than Spain or Italy. In the sixteenth century she was not, like Italy, bound up with the destiny of the Austrian empire, nor, like Spain, torn asunder by internal strife. Thus of all the so-called Latin nations she was the most capable of accepting a great heritage and developing it. Only a lover of shadows would regret what France might have given to literature and philosophy had she been resolute to follow the impulses of her racial genius alone. One can well imagine that this composite nation, so favorably placed in the rich territories of the Continent, would have produced some remarkable individuals and some interesting works; probably they would all have amounted to nothing compared with that unique thing in the modern world—French literature.

In order to understand what this literature has meant during the last four centuries one must try to picture French literature as a single personality.

I realize that the genius of a language and of a people is always more or less comparable to a human personality which is born, emerges from childhood, grows up, reaches maturity, the zenith, then wanes and dies. But this development often seems to be anarchic and casual. One notices, among those men who mark its stages, anomalies and asymmetries that are flagrant. There are often long periods of silence which are like eclipses of the genius of a nation. On the other hand, when one considers the life of the great thinker and writer whom I call "French literature," one is struck by the continuity of his effort, the good order of his experiments, the harmony of his history, and the logic of his development.

And so, round about the year 1548, France resolved to undertake a great work and to devote hundreds of years to the doing of it. All the Frenchmen who have been associated in this work have been conscious of the part they are playing in the whole and have accepted the strict discipline imposed on them by this majestic combination of effort.

What is this work of a whole nation? What is this monument with which French literature is associated? I should answer at once, a portrait of Man.

French literature has undertaken to depict man as he is, relentlessly; man individual, man social, the inner man and the outer man, man visible and man invisible, man subjective and man objective.

When we study works of art and their connecting links, we are struck by the regularity with which the labor has been accomplished, by shifts and by stages, through four centuries. Task succeeds task, and experience experience, as in a human life intelligently directed. French literature has behaved like a sensible person who travels prudently and always in the same direction.

Both thought and writing need a precise instrument; a language that is firm and sure. The first task of the great Frenchmen of the sixteenth century was to enrich and codify the language. I suspect that the word "codify" may make some people uncomfortable. I know that a language is a living thing which, like the people it expresses, must absorb nourishment and undergo change—must live, in fact—but French has managed to live, and still lives, without abandoning the strict rules that are the guarantee and the very condition of all creations of the mind.

The poets of the Pleiad have been accused of having introduced into the language a host of words of Greek origin, foreign to our phonetic genius. The reproach is futile. Have we retained more than two hundred words or roots from the original Gallic? The philologist reminds us that we do not even know how "yes" was said in Gallic. Spoken French has grown out of a number of different elements. Greek, from which either directly or via Latin we have received numerous roots, is one of the most important sources, and a source which is rich in bright tone-colors.

Most notable is the constant care taken by writers and poets and philosophers to perfect their instrument, to fix the rules and usage of grammar, to extend and purify the vocabulary, to specify spelling and establish punctuation. It is really surprising to realize nowadays that Corneille had to fight for u and v to be represented by two different letters. This passion for law and order is not an abuse. I have had in my hands editions of Malleville and Benserade in which the poet's names were spelled quite differently on different pages. It is interesting to watch the gradual codification of punctuation, too meagre with some authors, too plentiful with others (as, for example, with the abbé de Saint-Réal, who puts a comma after every other word); it is interesting, too, to note authors taking punctuation out of the hands of the compositors, and wielding themselves this important accessory of language and style.

Such pursuits are not, of course, the principal occupation of the creative minds which are the artisans of French genius; what is so striking is the unobtrusive way in which this teamwork is carried out, the mutual understanding, the dovetailing of the smaller perfections with the great works.

It may be desirable to try to discover a general trend in the mass of fact and fiction, but it would be a pity to diminish so glorious a page of human history by taking too systematic a view. The classical French writers and poets, while performing their important task of exploring the passions, endeavor to rediscover the guiding principles and laws of art, the laws established and tested by that antiquity which they admire and aim at perpetuating. Thus they restore what I should like to call the rule of economy and discipline.

If Shakespeare, incomparable poet, was barbarously treated by the French scholars of the seventeenth century, it was because their researches then led them very far from his adventurous genius. Our great writers were fascinated by the example of the Greeks and the Romans and yearned for literary bondage. They revived on the stage the three unities, they insisted on strict prosody in verse, and finally they set themselves to prove that their artistic principles of discipline and economy were borrowed from nature, which is not free, as it is mistakenly said to be, but is dominated by strict laws and stern necessities.

Can the austere classic art of Racine or Molière, which seems at first sight to be conventional and foreign to nature, possibly disclose the secret principles of animal and vegetable life? It is more than possible—it is certain. Almost all living beings instinctively practice economy and saving; instinctively all human beings know that, if they wish to live to accomplish their destiny and build lasting works, they must not spend all they possess but must put something to reserve. Man exists by robbing animals of their reserves of fat, vegetables of their reserves of sugar, all those humble provisions that life makes against famine. The peasant learns from the example of animals and plants and puts a similar economic law into practice. He learns to save. He builds granaries, silos, and reservoirs. He never spends all that he has. We may say he is a miser—but he is pre-eminently wise and natural.

Strange that the fundamental laws of our classic art enable us to understand the French peasant, whom the entire world is now reproaching for his practical qualities!

The writer in the classical tradition does not spend all he has, does not say all he knows, does not undertake more than he can carry out, does not shout louder than his voice allows, keeps some reserves, controls himself, makes rules, and obeys them. The romantic tradition, on the other hand, not only spends everything it has to give, but runs into debt.

My opponents may suggest that my thesis is untenable because it would suggest that in France romanticism has destroyed or endangered the classics. Of course I do not suggest this, because in its romantic wanderings French genius has kept its respect for traditional values and proved possessions. We know well enough that in France, even after the worst follies, even after the most violent lurches, there has always been someone to take the helm and guide the ship back to the middle of the stream.

II

DISCIPLINE

FRENCH literature is not a world of experiments in anarchy, but a society governed by strict rules, a Church, one and indivisible. The word "church" implies assembly, and it is as an assembly that I regard French literature. It is not in my view a haphazard meeting or an accidental collection of men and personalities. Across space and time it is seen as a harmonious group of men and their works, ordered and controlled by a broad and unique design.

I know that great men are only men, that great minds seldom think alike, and that they may seem to contradict this superior order I am trying to visualize. Bossuet is cruel to Molière, Malherbe treats Ronsard with scant respect, Pascal is hard on Montaigne, Rousseau in *Émile* tears La Fontaine to pieces with ferocious joy, Balzac in his correspondence shows the most violent scorn for Victor Hugo. Like children who quarrel among themselves but are nevertheless united when the time comes to stand by the family, the great writers do not hesitate to give vent to their disputes; but they unite in respect and obedience: respect for the language they serve, and for the destiny of the literature of which they are part, obedience to the rules established by centuries of labor.

There is no Church, no true assembly without discipline and obligations. It is strange that our French people, long famous for their faith in the individual, should have produced this remarkable community founded on observance and discipline. Thanks to this discipline French is still a unique language, at once popular and scholarly, avoiding the dangers of corruption by dialect; and thanks to this discipline the writers of four centuries ago are today immediately intelligible to the average man of moderate education.

The Churches, even the strictest of them, could not, except at their peril, deny the laws of life, that is to say movement and development. French literature has never ceased to develop new and splendid growths but has always been afraid of heretics and has always resisted them. There has been no crusade—hardly even a civil war; it seems rather that the people I am now calling heretics, apart from that especially favored and beloved *enfant terrible,* lyric poetry, have constantly been smothered by indifference and oblivion.

To whom should this formidable epithet "heretic" be applied? As far as French prose is concerned there can be no doubt. They are heretics who have left the beaten track, broad but well defined, of four hundred years of language and thought, all those who have tried to shine at the expense of others by frivolous experiments in schism and independent action which might deflect the true course of French thought and literature. It would be difficult to write a history of these heresies because, having been suppressed in embryo, they have no history. A few eccentrics of genius have succeeded in installing themselves on the frontiers of the literary empire—they have never succeeded in withdrawing from it entirely. Men of my generation came into the world of letters at a time when disruptive influences were at work. We know now that these experiments have proved to be without a future. The style of Péladan, or even of Paul Adam and some others, has not obtained the assent of the council, and the work of these writers, despite undoubted merits, seems henceforward to be excommunicated.

I can well imagine how such a remark might wound the young men who bring to literature an ardent desire for regeneration. I appreciate and sympathize with this desire, because life is a dull and unprofitable thing without it; but I know from experience that the Church of French literature has always required of genius, even the most original genius, that it should observe her laws and respect her history and traditions. The mysterious thing is that through this subjection, voluntarily and finally accepted, our great writers have arrived at an effective principle of power.

If we wish to estimate the severity of the restriction we have only to consider the sort of reservation made by the literary Church—I am pursuing the metaphor—in respect of various regional tendencies in literature. I am not passing judgment on the phenomenon—it is not attributable, of course, to any deliberate plan, but to instinctive forces. Regional literature throughout France, before admittance to the Church, has had to accept her ritual; that is to say, to honor the one and indivisible French language, except for occasional eccentricities of vocabulary and syntax. This homage rendered, the works of enduring value have been carried away from their local habitation to be inscribed in the national treasure. Flaubert's and Maupassant's Normandy is first and foremost France; Mauriac's Gascony is already annexed. Authors who come to ask for a Paris imprimatur understand all this well enough.

French literature owns several provinces outside the borders of France which are not exempt from the common law. These provinces have some good writers and have made notable contributions to the common treasure. May they be obedient like us, and may they subscribe to no major heresy! For when they throw off the yoke of the Church they renounce her privileges too.

And the privileges are great, in return for this rigorous service. Everyone who uses the French language experiences simultaneously the discipline and the joy of communion. The writer especially must be more aware than anyone else of the humility and pride of his state, and if he has not the feeling when he takes up his pen of writing under the watchful and severe but friendly eye of an assembly of honored predecessors and worthy peers, then, in my opinion, he is renouncing both the duties and the essential advantages of his calling.

III

L'ENFANT TERRIBLE

THE rigorous observance and discipline, the rule of the Church of French literature which so many great writers have followed faithfully, has always been waived in favor of lyric poetry.

In the most strictly brought up families there is usually one rebellious child who cannot adapt himself to the family law, a child tenderly loved but not properly understood, criticized, but tolerated with all his whims and tempers and extravagances.

Such has been the fate of lyric poetry in the French literary family. It has been, and still is, in France the spoiled child and darling, sometimes the prodigal child, sometimes the accursed child—but always forgiven.

This odd state of affairs has not been properly understood by scholars, especially abroad. The oratorical splendor of a literature dedicated to the interpretation of men and the world and founded in order and discipline, seems to have dazzled many critics and induced them to take too simple a view. It has been said, and is still said in other countries, that France has no lyric poets at all, and that French, unlike English or German, is not a suitable medium for lyrical effusions. This is a very arbitrary judgment. The miracle is precisely that French, notwithstanding its splendidly luminous and analytical qualities, has always been responsive to the demands of the poets, and has proved to be an incomparably supple and musical instrument in their hands.

For centuries the best minds have been engaged in making French an unrivaled instrument of precision and analysis, but that has not prevented lyric poetry from flourishing on the side. I say "on the side"; in the great century the middle of the stage was held by dramatic poetry, first cousin to lyric poetry, with which it shared duties and responsibilities; but lyricism has never lost its position. In a preface to an anthology of French lyric poetry I pointed out that the extreme difficulty of our lyric poetry is not due to some rare disease of the imagination, but is a veritable tradition, handed down from the fifteenth century to our times and renewed among the symbolists of today.

It is interesting to remark that the Frenchman, naturally a logician and a grammarian, has always admitted certain dispensations in favor of poetry, poetic licenses in fact. It is gratifying to see such licenses conceded to an art which in other respects is strictly and even absurdly regulated. Poetry is the prodigious prodigal son, the delicate monster. And so French lyricism has won wide acceptance by scholars, in folklore, and in our heritage of popular songs. Molière, right in the middle of the most disciplined period, honors folklore on the stage, and it is curious to hear the Misanthrope reciting verses which were then being sung, and had been sung for a long time, by the common folk.

This agreement to differ between the literary family

and the poet, the spoiled darling and *enfant terrible,* seems to have been suspended by romanticism. During this extraordinary period we see poetry reinstated in the normal literary stream. Perhaps it would be more accurate to say that we see the normal stream overflowing its banks into the territories of lyricism. Immediately romanticism is exhausted the divorce becomes operative again. The whole symbolist movement grows in mysterious shadow, outside the main literary currents in which the tradition of thought and language is embodied.

Therefore let us have no heretics in the French literary Church; no heretics except poets. I find it right that it should be so, right that the poet should be free, a little outside the Church militant, that he should sometimes receive her protection and her consolation, that he should be sometimes chastised but finally acclaimed, that he should represent the divine and redeeming exception. I believe it is proper that the long triumph of order and reason should be secretly troubled by the noble faults of ecstasy; and I find it excellent that poetic madness, in constantly threatening the equilibrium of the ship, should effectively remind us all of what equilibrium is, and of our need of it.

IV

CLARITY AND MODERATION

FOR what is the equilibrium of an organism in movement except a perpetual struggle to restore the balance of conflicting forces and to create a harmony that is the fairer for being unstable and uncertain?

Once in my presence a man who knew both France and America well advised some French tourists who were about to cross the ocean, never on the other side to use such discredited expressions as "measure, clarity, order, or Cartesian logic." I know very well that these ideas, only too easily abstract, have suffered a certain amount of didactic abuse. To offer foreigners a tiresome and slightly ridiculous picture and to overstress our greatest qualities, our clarity, for example, would be a great blunder, perhaps a disaster, and would be most damaging to this very quality.

What exactly is this celebrated French clarity which has been admired for so long and which cannot be laughed at with impunity?

I remember one day having delivered a lecture to a German audience, a lecture which I had carefully prepared and constructed according to our classical rules. As I was leaving the platform a university professor, an excellent scholar, said: "You are a real Frenchman!

We Germans, instead of beginning, as you did, by rapidly outlining the scope and the divisions of the subject, would have begun by casting a little shadow round it." This remark is strangely reminiscent of one of Mallarmé's celebrated utterances. But Mallarmé was a poet, and the poet, even in France, has royal privileges. It is true to say that almost all French writers have used the French language as an instrument whose proper function is to classify ideas and states of mind and to render them intelligible.

That is a great and a worthy undertaking. If it is admitted, in principle, that man is made for knowledge and that he can do nothing better than know, then we should praise those people who make a methodical and exacting and determined effort in the first place to understand exactly what they think and afterwards to comprehend what the objective world has to offer them. And if knowledge needs the light, then let there be light, and may that light shine through our work!

Is it possible that excess of clarity may operate against the needs of perfect knowledge? It is possible. An excess of light can be dazzling. Therein lies a danger to the mind from which the real artists escape at the right moment by drawing a veil, or interposing a screen, or evoking a cloud. It is also possible that the full light of day may be not only blinding but corrosive and destructive and that it may destroy both the color and the texture of the materials exposed to its action. A skillful and resourceful artist can feel this instinctively. Needless to say the scholar and the artist do not make the same use of the light, and by analogy do not employ language in the same way.

In the most successful works of our national treasure, clarity may sometimes give a feeling, especially to foreigners, of avarice and parsimony, in respect of the object under illumination.

Beware of hasty judgments on this difficult question. The role of language is to "resolve" at all costs, for our peace of mind and irrespective of our wishes. To resolve at all costs for the final salvation of mankind, even when, the operation done, we are going to think with a touch of disappointment, "So it was nothing but that! And so that is all that is left us!"

Before asserting that any page of the great book of France is too clear, let us assure ourselves that we have fully savored it, completely grasped its meaning. Lovers of the shade are often inclined to declare the world empty because they are incapable of seeing anything, because they cannot appreciate perfect nakedness. French psychologists and writers have gone as far in the knowledge of man and nature as they can go without compromise and ambiguity, and without counting on the good graces of luck and the powers of darkness.

Zealous propagandists spread the idea freely that France is, *par excellence,* the country of moderation. To hear them one would think that the hillsides of the Île de France and Touraine were the only hillsides in the world, and that the view from these marvelous hillsides would suffice to imbue the soul of the inhabitants with a miraculous sense of moderation and just proportion and reasonable action. Do not let us trust this rather "Tainian" sentimentality. The history of France proves again and again that the most charming geographical emotions are not sufficient to give rise to political and social wisdom. The country of moderation has had more revolutions than any other European country. It has not, so far as I know, always been a model of prudence and balance. Passions and crimes and sins work their havoc in France as elsewhere. And if France may be proud of the valleys of Normandy and the landscapes of Poitiers, she also possesses wild mountains, desolate plains, rushing torrents, and barren heaths. No, let us guard against this vain and ridiculous eloquence. But let us remember that through her language and her literature, through the untiring energy of her civilized minds, France through the ages has at least made a praiseworthy effort to arrive at moderation. France is not yet, alas, the country of moderation; but she is the country where the master minds have made the most genuine efforts, through their works, to teach respect for moderation.

V

MORALS AND HUMANISTS

Is French literature, as it used to be said, a literature of moralists? Here is a problem that needs examination.

The word "moralist" in days gone by used to connote observer and recorder of morals and manners. Without losing its original sense it has gradually taken on that of moralizer. Will French literature, the literature of moralists, become a literature of moralizers?

The majority of the great French writers have described the manners of their time and have proceeded thence to show the way of life of mankind in general, claiming by their descriptions to work for the betterment of the species. Ethical preoccupation is inevitably part of such literature, and the result is that the words "moral" and "moralist" take on a wider meaning. From La Fontaine to Molière and Voltaire this impulse to control manners and customs has characterized all the leading writers of our literature. Destouches is quite candid about it. He says: "I believe that dramatic art is worthy only when it aims at instruction through entertainment." The impulse was often adventitious. Our masters followed their desire, which was to depict; and to justify this desire they made a pious pretense of having nothing in view except the perfection of man-

kind. We are at liberty to doubt the motive without in
the least slighting the genius of these artists. However
that may be, the avowed pretext was for a long time a
moral, or rather an ethical one. Let us note this in
order properly to understand the tendencies of the new
century.

There is no writer worthy of the name who does not
want to exercise influence. There is no writer who does
not believe that his influence is salutary. Even the
cynics themselves, when they publish their outbursts,
affirm with touching candor their wish to work for the
well-being of mankind. The madmen who dream of
disorder and destruction are doubtless persuaded, in
the bottom of their hearts, that annihilation is a desirable, and in fact a moral, solution for mankind. Most
writers, because they work constructively whether for
good or ill, necessarily proclaim an optimistic faith. We
are forced to believe that they refuse allegiance to noth-
ingness, and that they say with Sénancour, "L'homme
est périssable. Il se peut; mais périssons en résistant, et,
si le néant nous est réservé, ne faisons pas que ce soit
une justice." [1]

Of course I do not disapprove of the wish expressed
by so many writers—whether sincerely or not—to improve behavior and to better mankind. It seems to me,
however, that the writers of the twentieth century express this wish less frequently than their predecessors,
and I do not blame them. One important reason for

---

[1] Miguel de Unamuno, who liked this phrase, told me one day that
he would have preferred it to read as follows: "Faisons que ce ne soit
pas une justice." Unamuno was a great believer in the power of the
will. I approve his version, while modifying it slightly to the form
"Faisons que ce ne soit pas justice."

this development is to be found in the change in public morality. I do not think that morals are lower today than yesterday or that licentiousness is more tolerated. I believe, like everyone else, that a greater liberty of writing is admissible, at any rate in France. The recorder of manners and morals has no longer any need to search for a pretext or an excuse. Choderlos de Laclos wrote in the preface to *Les Liaisons dangereuses:* "It seems to me, putting it at its lowest, that it is a service to morals to expose the methods used by the wicked to corrupt the good." Self-deception! Laclos does not care a rap for rendering "a service to morals." He is concerned only with observing them and portraying them, and I notice that he is more interested and curious, happier perhaps, the more the spectacle is improper and cruel. But still he thinks it prudent to invoke the classic excuse. He does so very superficially, and it is obviously only as a matter of form.

Nowadays we can afford to dispense with this hypocrisy and illusion. For the idea of instruction there is gradually being substituted the stricter and sadder and purer idea of knowledge. The writer of the twentieth century portrays morals in order to make an act of knowledge, to bear witness at the tribunal of humanity. If his evidence happens to be of some effect in reforming some people, well, the writer does not object to such a beneficial result.

We may, and we should, hope that the stories of the novelists and the dissertations of the essayists, the cries or the songs of the poets, will have a favorable effect on the moral life. It remains to consider along what lines such an effect may operate.

I do not suppose that it can be possible to effect any profound change in the physiological and moral habits of man, the finished article. We can interest a man when he is in the prime of life, make him reconsider his reasons, shake his beliefs, disturb his leisure, perhaps even help him in his orientation if the wind is blowing in the right direction. We can amuse him or attract him, or, conversely, annoy him and disappoint him. Perhaps it is just possible to move him a little in the direction of his powerful, instinctive, and sentimental forces, but I doubt whether it is possible appreciably to change a fully matured man, either by force of argument or by description, or by eloquence, or by the music of words, or by all these elements combined.

It is not at all the same with young and malleable minds, which are capable of receiving and retaining new impressions. In the moral sphere one can exert a great and a lasting influence on children. The essential influence of a writer is not that which he exerts immediately on the public by the first distribution of his works, it is what he exercises, even unknown to himself, through the intermediary of teachers and scholars on the children of the generations to come. I realize fully that one must first be accepted by the teachers, and that their intelligent understanding must be enlisted in order to obtain their mediatory action and collaboration. Because of this function teachers are always in the front row of the audience; they preserve, even in maturity, the freshness and vivacity of the youth whom it is their duty to instruct.

Thanks to the assistance of teachers, writers find eventually their best response among their remotest public, which is the final justification for a work of art.

This presupposes a friendly and continuously active collaboration between practical and scholarly literature, between the literary world and the university. Such collaboration we should not have dared to hope for thirty years ago. Alarmed by the excesses of realism and the alchemy of the symbolists the university showed extreme distrust, or at least a frowning reserve, towards living literature—by which I mean the literature of living writers. It was a time when the literary manuals in use in the schools made only a derisive mention of Baudelaire, who is now honored among us as a god of the written word. It was a time when the life of French literature appeared to the student to stop dead at the beginning of the nineteenth century.

Such a state of affairs could not have lasted without serious danger to all concerned. Enthusiasm and anger were aroused simultaneously among the keen young intelligentsia by the paradox that authors whom the French universities insisted on misunderstanding or belittling figured in the courses of all the schools of Romance languages abroad and furnished subjects for theses to university students in Scandinavia and America.

Things have changed very much for the better in literature. The university of our day, under the control of broad-minded men, has shown that criticism affirms its power and assumes its highest responsibilities in applying itself courageously to contemporary work. In all departments of the university numbers of qualified teachers have begun to illuminate their teaching by comparison of ancient and modern, and to accept the assistance of present-day minds in explaining the world around us.

Whether the writer admits or pretends to despise the function of instructor and teacher there is another role of which, however skeptical he is, he cannot think without tenderness. Many writers who have no intention of being guides and philosophers are really, and they know it themselves, comforters and friends. I am not misusing words. There is no consolation for our deepest sorrows. Nevertheless, let us try to imagine what existence would be like without reading, let us estimate the grip that trouble, sorrow, sickness or any other adversity would have over us. Even in its most despairing melodies art is a living work. Even when it portrays fatality, suffering and death, art is light and life. Because it interests us in life, art is very near making us love life. If only because it helps us to endure life, art deserves our gratitude.

It is quite obvious that French literature, in its contemporary adventures, is not far removed from its illustrious traditions. The great discourse on man, as it develops, naturally becomes also a discourse for man. The work of the humanists from century to century is fulfilled in human work. That this precious treasure may be enriched and increased is the fervent wish of all good men. Do not let us forget that the treasure is in our hands and that we are responsible. Let us love it and honor it as our surest wealth, our inalienable possession, our bread for the days to come.

FINIS